The
Medical Society of London
1773-1973

The Founders' Picture by Samuel Medley, 1800

The
Medical Society of London
1773-1973

Edited by Thomas Hunt, C.B.E.

John Coakley Lettsom, M.D., F.R.S. (From a wax medallion in the
possession of Mr. John H. A. Elliott, great-great-grandson of Dr. Lettsom).

Published for The Medical Society of London
by WILLIAM HEINEMANN MEDICAL BOOKS LTD
LONDON

First Published 1972

© 1972 The Medical Society of London

ISBN 0 433 15670 8

M HH 3 6
25/7/80

Printed in Great Britain by
The Whitefriars Press Ltd. London and Tonbridge

Contents

List of Illustrations

Preface

SIR V. ZACHARY COPE

The Medical Society of London was founded in 1773, two years before the outbreak of the American War of Independence. It was the first regularly constituted general medical society to be formed in England and to understand its far-reaching influence upon the development of the medical profession in the country it is necessary briefly to examine the state of the profession at that time.

In 1773 there were three groups of men who were usually called upon to treat the sick and injured—the physicians, the surgeons and the apothecaries. None of these three groups associated freely with the others.

The physicians were either Fellows or Licentiates of the Royal College of Physicians of London and most of them practised in or near London; a few "Extra" Licentiates practised in one or other of the larger English cities or towns. In order to qualify for the Fellowship of the College a man had first to graduate in Arts at Oxford or Cambridge University and then spend several years studying medicine at the same university; little clinical work was required of him. To shorten the time of study some men took degrees in Arts and Medicine at a continental university, then took a medical degree at Oxford or Cambridge and then presented themselves at the College to be examined for a Fellowship. At any one time until the nineteenth century the number of Fellows of the College was seldom much over fifty. Licentiates of the College had to have acquired considerable clinical experience, either as an apprentice or as pupil at a hospital and at examination they had to show that they had studied the works of Galen and had a good knowledge of drugs. Only three or four Licentiates were admitted each year and they took no part in the management of the College.

In 1745 an Act of Parliament authorised the surgeons to separate themselves from the Barber-Surgeons' Company and to form The Company of Surgeons. The period of apprenticeship was maintained and an examination in anatomy and surgery was required before a candidate became a member of the Company. Experience in military or naval surgery might shorten the period of apprenticeship, so that the number of surgeons considerably increased.

The third and largest group was that of the apothecaries who in 1617 had been granted a charter by James I to form The Worshipful Company of Apothecaries. The apothecaries at first sold drugs and made up prescriptions for the physicians but soon they began to give advice as well. In 1703 the House of Lords decided that apothecaries could give advice gratuitously but could only charge for medicaments provided. The number of physicians (Fellows and Licentiates) was very limited while the number of apothecaries, in spite of their long apprenticeship, grew continually in London and in many parts of the country. The College of Physicians tried hard to repress the apothecaries and there was continual friction between the two bodies which was sometimes very bitter.

John Coakley Lettsom, who took a leading part in the formation of the Medical Society of London, had been for some years an apprentice to an able apothecary in Settle, Yorkshire and was well acquainted with the unsatisfactory state of medical affairs in England and particularly in London. He was a friendly man and a Quaker. It must have been due to him that, in July and August 1773, the Society passed two laws which laid down (1) that the Council of the Society shall consist of three physicians, three surgeons and three apothecaries and (2) that the number of members of the Society shall be limited to thirty physicians, thirty surgeons and thirty apothecaries.

Thus the constitution of the Society proclaimed the equality of the three groups and encouraged friendliness between

members. After this time disputes between the physicians and
the apothecaries became less bitter and the relaxation of
surgical apprenticeship for those who had acted as surgeons in
naval or military warfare made it possible for many apothecaries to qualify in surgery more easily.

A quarrel in 1805 caused some members of the Medical
Society of London to leave and form the Medico-Chirurgical
Society, but this did not divert the original society from its
main purpose. During the nineteenth century the extent of
medical knowledge greatly increased and many societies were
formed in London for the study of special subjects, but the
Medical Society of London preserved a wide outlook and carefully chose recent and up-to-date subjects for discussion. Thus
when Joseph Lister came from Edinburgh to London, in order
to convince the London surgeons of the value of the antiseptic
treatment of wounds, he chose the Medical Society of London
to make known his views on several occasions. As Godlee wrote
in his Life of Lord Lister—"The Medical Society, the doyen
of the group, formed by Fothergill and Lettsom in 1773, seems
to have been a particular favourite for him as was shown by
his bequest to them of the pick of his medical library. He
delivered the annual oration in 1891 and spoke on at least
three others. One address dealt with coagulation of the blood,
two with antiseptic dressings, and the fourth was on the burning
question of the open treatment of fracture of the patella".

The memorable occasion when Lister demonstrated patients
on whom he had operated on the broken patella with silver
wire was vividly described by Sir St. Clair Thomson at the
Society's meeting on 9th October 1939:

"The President's reference to antiseptics had a peculiar
and personal reference to him. He was Lister's house-
surgeon at the time and it was his part to collect the cases
for demonstration. In all Lister had operated on seven cases
of fracture of the patella. All of these cases were published
and six out of seven of the patients were present in this very
room at the meeting of the Society. He recollected well the

astonishment with which the members of the Society tried to feel the silver wire. Some were aghast at the unwarrantable danger in the opening of a healthy knee-joint, for at that date a healthy joint was regarded, as Erichsen said in 1874 of the abdomen and brain, as "forever shut to the wise and humane surgeon."

Only two junior surgeons from King's College Hospital, Royce Bell and William Rose—and two junior surgeons from another school (Astley Bloxam) welcomed the communication, endorsing the treatment advised and quoting their results.

Others said that the majority of such cases could get along without operation although they might require six months' rest. One hospital surgeon, Morrant Baker, asked "Had not ankylosis, suppuration and death been heard of after this operation?" Another surgeon asked that if the next case died Lister should be prosecuted for malpractice, while one exclaimed dramatically "C'est magnifique, mais ce n'est pas la chirurgie". (*Transactions* for 1939).

The above account shows medical discussion at its liveliest, and Lister's demonstration must have convinced all young surgeons who read the description in the societys' *Transactions*.

When, in 1907, the Medico-Chirurgical Society joined with many other medical societies to form the Royal Society of Medicine, which had many sections, each representing a group of doctors specially interested in a special department of medicine, the Medical Society of London did not think it wise to join the new society, one of the chief principles of foundation of the older society being to cater for, and be governed by, representatives of medicine, surgery and general practice; incidentally, fifty years passed before the new society formed a special section for those in general practice. The Royal Society of Medicine has during the last half-century developed into a famous institution with many thousands of Fellows; it has many sections, each largely autonomous but represented on the general Council. It has a vast library and a splendid library service with a photographic section. Its meetings are recorded and printed in the well edited Proceedings.

The Medical Society of London, on the other hand, has continued its original function—to provide a regular series of meetings, with discussions on every branch of medicine or surgery, for an audience of both general practitioners and specialists. The Council of the Society is very careful in its choice of subjects for discussion, the various papers and some of the discussions being recorded in its *Tranactions*, of which a copy is sent to every member of the Society.

The twentieth century has already seen more important advances in every branch of medicine and surgery than any previous epoch and there is clearly a need not only for a comprehensive society which shall include sections for the intensive study of each branch of the healing art, but also smaller societies that arrange to pass on to members—whether general practitioners or consultants—conclusions that can be applied in practice. The Medical Society of London has done this for two centuries and I believe and hope that it may long continue to fulfil this most useful function.

Acknowledgements

I am most grateful to those who have generously allowed us to use illustrations and to Miss Ann Mitchell for her help in selecting and arranging them. The Royal College of Physicians have allowed us to reproduce a number of portraits from their collection, and the Wellcome Museum have also helped us especially by permitting us to use the "Conversation Piece" of Lettsom and his family by a follower of Devis (previously attributed to Zoffany) which hangs in their museum. Heinemann Medical Books have kindly allowed us to use some of the illustrations which appeared in "Lettsom" written by J. Johnston Abraham, and his daughter Mrs. Martin has allowed us to photograph the original account sent by Lettsom which appears on Page 12. The Trustees of the British Museum supplied the photographs of old London and the map, on Pages 6, 114, 117, and Miss Olive Monahan, formerly Matron of the Margate Sea Bathing Hospital very kindly gave us the photograph of the Hospital reproduced on Page 49.

Introduction by the Editor

When the Council of the Medical Society of London decided upon a number of commemorative actions to mark the occasion of its 200th Anniversary, if the most noticeable of these was the alteration and redecoration of its House in Chandos Street, the publication of some history of the Society's past personalities and activities was certainly no less called for.

I was invited to edit such a volume and I am deeply grateful to those Fellows of the Society who have written about the activities of the Society and the men who played leading parts in its 200 years' existence. No attempt has been made to produce a full and definitive history, but I most fully appreciate the amount of work these authors have given to studying our past records, and the willing co-operation and enthusiasm which they have shown in selecting aspects of our history which they felt to be of the greatest interest. Where there has been overlapping of subject-matter between various contributors I have made some exclusions or exchanges in order to make the whole contents read more smoothly, and it is particularly generous of the authors to have allowed me to make these alterations in their texts, for which I accept responsibility. I, and many of the contributors, owe much to the classic biography of Lettsom by J. Johnson Abraham (a past Lloyd Roberts Lecturer) which ranges over many fields of seventeenth and eighteenth century life.

It is particularly happy that Sir V. Zachary Cope, who has been a Fellow and Hon. Fellow of the Society for over fifty years and was President in 1939, should have written a Preface. We are most grateful to the Trustees of the Wellcome Foundation who, by their generous offer of financial help if necessary, encouraged us to go forward with our project.

The Society began at a time when great changes in medical and social life were taking place. At its Centenary dinner in 1873 the then President commented on such new developments as the microscope and clinical thermometer. Today, at our Bicentenary, changes are again taking place which markedly affect the role of such societies as ours. One such change has been the admission of Lady Fellows for the first time, and another the rapid and widespread increase of "official" postgraduate lectures, meetings and symposia, so that "private" Medical Society meetings have assumed a different importance from that of twenty years ago.

It is a great satisfaction to the Society that the sale of some of its old books—many are already housed on loan at the Wellcome Historical Library—is likely to lead to the formation of an Institute of Medical History in Canada. So this 200th Anniversary will mark a renewal of the link with that continent to which many of Lettsom's "dissenting" colleagues had emigrated and where he had many friends and associations.

Amongst those who have helped in the production of this volume our thanks are especially due to Major Mitchell, Registrar of the Society, Miss Ann Mitchell who has been responsible for the illustrations, Mrs. Johnson who has assisted with the editorial work and particularly Mr. Emery of William Heinemann Medical Books for his skilled advice and assistance.

September, 1972   Thomas Hunt

Chapter I

Dr. Lettsom and the Foundation of the Society

THOMAS HUNT

The reign of George III (1760–1820) covered a period of great social change in Great Britain at the same time as the Encyclopaedists were changing attitudes in most countries of Europe. In 1773 Diderot visited the Empress Catherine in St. Petersburg, and by 1780 the last of the 34 volumes of his *Encyclopedie* was published, spreading a message of atheism and revolt. There was a growing sense of social conscience. In 1772 a judgement of Lord Mansfield laid down that the status of slavery was inadmissible on English soil. In 1781 Dr. Thomas Percival, a Nonconformist physician, founded the Manchester Library and Philosophical Society, which concerned itself with subjects such as the appalling housing conditions of the poor, the hours of labour in factories, and the almost total disregard for the health and nutrition of working people. Writers in 1773—the year in which the Medical Society of London was founded—reported "the unhappy progress of Rickets among us" and Fordyce observed that "there must be very near twenty-thousand children in London and Westminster and their suburbs, ill at this moment of the Hectic Fever, attended with tun-bellies, swelled wrists and ankles, or crooked limbs". In 1775 an Act was passed for the registration and inspection of private madhouses and for reform of abuses in the prisons. In parliament a motion was carried that "the influence of the Crown has increased, is increasing and ought to be diminished".

But though the spirit of reform was spreading, the anti-Popery (Gordon) riots of 1779 (see Prisons, Ch. III) showed that religious bitterness still ran very deep. In times of such violent conflict the Quakers played an important role. In 1776 their brethren in North America signed the Declaration of Independence, declaring the thirteen colonies a Republic. Bostonians protested against the tea duty by staging the Boston Tea Party (1773); and Philadelphia founded its splendid museum. Farther afield, Captain Cook was successfully sailing round the world (1772-5), thanks to Lind's recommendation to give his crew oranges and lemons and thus prevent scurvy. The Industrial Revolution was in progress and new manufactured goods such as calico were produced for the first time. In the year of our Society's foundation, Oliver Goldsmith wrote *She stoops to Conquer*, Haydn his *Stabat Mater*, and Reynolds painted his famous "Lady Cockburn and her Children" and "The Graces decorating Hymen".

In the medical world, Quakers such as Fothergill and Lettsom were showing a spirit of kindliness and cooperation in treating the sick—an approach very different from the brusque tradition handed on from Radcliffe. With this new approach came the wish to discuss and compare patients and their illnesses and a change from "coffee-house consultations" to meetings of medical men in societies. In Europe the same thing was happening; in France the Royal Society of Medicine was established by Council and King in 1776, while in Germany the Imperial Leopoldine Academy was becoming an influential medical force. In Edinburgh, already one of the most famous medical schools in Europe, an early medical group had been formed by Monro Primus in 1732, publishing five volumes of *Essays and Observations;* in 1783 it became the Royal Society of Edinburgh, while another medical society in the city, founded in 1737, became the Royal Medical Society. Dr. John Fothergill was a member of this society, having taken his M.D. at Edinburgh in 1736 before coming to London in 1740. There, in 1752, he founded The Medical Society, soon to be called the Society of Physicians. This met on alternate Mondays at the

Mitre Tavern in Fleet Street, its members being "such as had the care of Hospitals or were otherwise in some degree of repute in their profession"; at one time it consisted only of seven physicians, six of whom were Fellows of the Royal Society. In 1764 a similar society was formed in London, restricted to licentiates of the College of Physicians and known as the Society of Licentiate Physicians. This also met fortnightly at Old Slaughter's Coffee House and dined once a quarter at the Crown and Anchor Tavern in the Strand. Since, by a rule of Charles II, dissenters were not admitted to the College, the society excluded a considerable body of physicians as well as all apothecaries and surgeons. Two other societies came into being in London just before Lettsom's foundation of the Medical Society of London: the Physical Society at Guy's Hospital (1771) and the Physico-Medical Society (also 1771) which, after an abortive attempt to unite with Lettsom's society, seems to have disappeared after only a few years.

Our Society was first known as the Society in Crane Court, later as the Society in Bolt Court. It was unique in representing the medical profession as a whole—30 physicians, 30 surgeons, and 30 apothecaries—and within twenty years doctors in different parts of the country began to follow its example. In Oxford a society for the promotion of medical knowledge was founded in 1780, meeting each week during the winter months in the Radcliffe Infirmary. The Middlesex Hospital Medical Society appeared in 1774; in 1779 the Great Queen Street Medical Society, linked to the School of Anatomy, was founded but survived only until about 1788. In 1782 Dr. S. F. Simmons, who attended George III during one of his periods of insanity and had been president of the Medical Society of London, left to found a new one of his own. This lasted only a year or two, by which time the remarkable Dr. George Fordyce had founded another, the Society for the Improvement of Medical and Chirurgical Knowledge (1783). John Hunter was closely associated with Fordyce in this venture, although his chief interest was in the Lyceum Medicum Londinense. This held Friday evening meetings at his anatomy school, which then stretched from his own great house in Leicester Square to what is now the Charing Cross Road, and was mainly an educational society, with a large number of student members. After some twenty years it merged with the Westminster Medical Society, finally joining with the Medical Society of London in 1851.

Thus the Medical Society of London was not only a pioneer in its ideals of promoting contact between the various fields of the medical world, but also among the few such societies to survive and flourish. And for this we must thank its remarkable founder Lettsom.

John Coakley Lettsom was born on November 22nd 1744 on the island of Little Vandyke in the West Indies. He was said to be one of seven pairs of male twins born to a hard-working Quaker planter who grew sugar and cotton in Tortola and an Irish mother descended from the Coakleys, baronets in Ireland. He came to England as a boy of six, went to the Quaker School at Penketh and was apprenticed at 16 to a surgeon and apothecary at Settle in Yorkshire. As an apprentice he soon began to visit patients and became absorbed in the study of botany, mineralogy and Latin. In the summer of 1766 Lettsom achieved his ambition of coming to London, arriving aged 21 with an introduction to the great Dr. John Fothergill, then one of the best-known physicians in Europe. Fothergill arranged for him to be entered as a surgeon's dresser at St. Thomas's Hospital, where he himself had been a student. One of the physicians there was Mark Akenside, a Court Physician and a notable poet, who was a regular contributor to Fothergill's newly-founded Society of Licentiate Physicians. Once a week, while working at St. Thomas's, Lettsom breakfasted with Fothergill and became more and more closely associated with the Quaker community in London. Since Friends' Meetings took place three or four times a week, work and religion seem to have filled his time. For a year Lettsom lived at 40 Gracechurch Street in the Borough, where St. Thomas's then was, after which, partly owing to lack of money, he stayed for two years with Dr. Fothergill in Cheshire before sailing for Tortola, where he arrived, after two months at sea, in December 1767.

There he started medical practice and within six months had made nearly £2,000. He had also inherited some ten or more slaves from his father's estate, worth at that time £400 to £500, but in characteristic Quaker spirit he freed them at once and so lost the much-needed residue of his patrimony. Before leaving Tortola for the last time in 1768, however, Lettsom bought two young slaves, Sam and Tom, for £200. He took Sam as his servant to England, where "black boys" were then

FIG. 1. John Coakley Lettsom 1744–1815.

6

fashionable, but freed Teresa, Sam's sister in 1782 and finally gave the "boys" their freedom too. He described himself as "The volatile Creole" and had a yellow complexion; he was tall and spare and sober, but his eyes sparkled with animation and humour.

After a short period in Edinburgh, where he came under the influence of William Cullen, Lettsom went on a tour of Europe —then almost obligatory for any cultivated young physician. At the end of his tour—mostly in France—he stayed for a time

FIG. 2. A map of the City of London showing Aldersgate Street (1) and Basinghall Street (2) (1791) (*British Museum*).

at Leyden, obtaining his M.D. degree there in 1769 with a
dissertation in Latin on the medicinal properties of tea. Later
this was amended and published in English (1772 and 1799)—
an indication of the considerable interest at that time in the
subject of tea-drinking; Dr. Johnson strongly supported the
habit, while John Wesley and many Nonconformists violently
opposed it. In 1770 Lettsom obtained the license of the Royal
College of Physicians, and in the same year married Ann
Miers, a wealthy heiress, at the Friends' Meeting House,
Devonshire Place. After his marriage he lived first in Great
Eastcheap, near Cannon Street, then at Sambrook Court,
No. 24 Basinghall Street—now the Wool Exchange—where he
practised until his death. Basinghall Street ran past the
Guildhall from Cheapside up Old Jury towards what is now
Moorgate Station, only a short walk from Aldersgate. In 1773
Lettsom was appointed second physician to the Aldersgate or
General Dispensary, one of the first charities to provide free
medical and surgical help for the poor. The same year he
published his "Reflections on the General Treatment and Cure
of Fevers", for which much of the material was said to have
been taken, without permission, from his old teacher Cullen.
"The Naturalists' and Travellers' Companion", which first
appeared in 1772, had a considerable success and was reprinted
and translated into Latin and German two years later—the
year that Priestley discovered oxygen. In 1773, aged 29,
Lettsom was elected a Fellow of the Royal Society—and he
founded the Medical Society of London.

His rapid rise to success is not hard to understand against
the medical background of the day. Lettsom, unlike society in
general and many doctors, was gentle and good-mannered.
Not only was there an enormous trade in quack medicine, but
dishonesty among the unqualified practitioners flourished in a
climate of credulity and widespread superstition. Drunkenness
was common among rich and poor alike—Rowlandson's paintings of the evils of gin-drinking do not exaggerate. The apothecaries rarely mixed with the few consultants who held the
licence of the Royal College of Physicians to practise within

seven miles of London and there was little idea of hygiene, sanitation, or care for public health. The government gave little thought to the poor, the destitute or the insane, and conditions in poor-houses, prisons and asylums were appalling, even by eighteenth-century standards. It was the Quakers who did most to arouse the public conscience, and Lettsom became

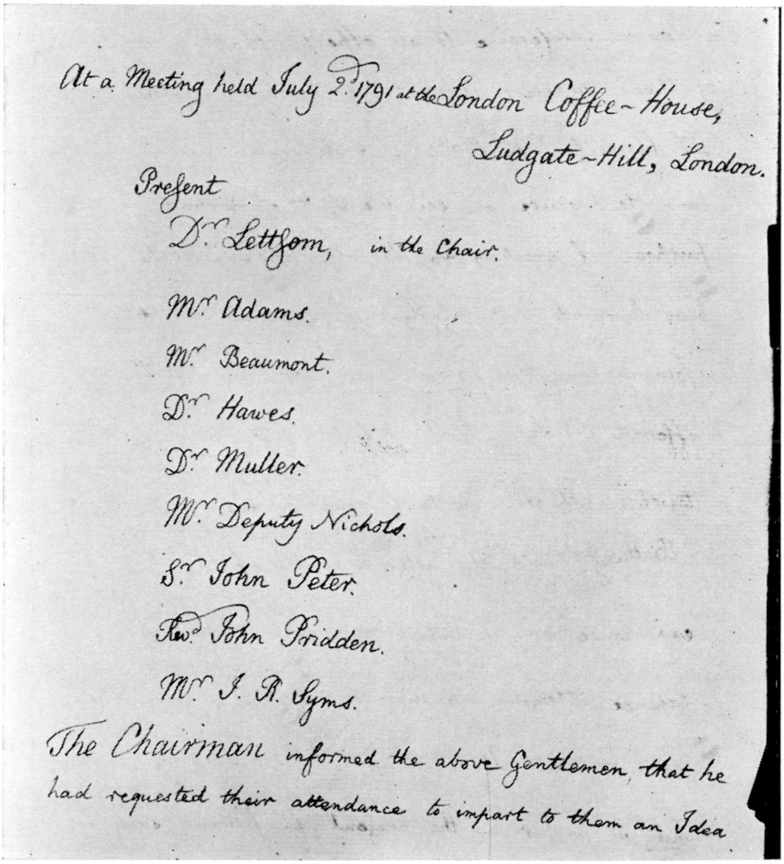

At a Meeting held July 2d 1791 at the London Coffee-House,
Ludgate-Hill, London.
Present
Dr Lettsom, in the Chair.
Mr Adams.
Mr Beaumont.
Dr Hawes.
Dr Muller.
Mr Deputy Nichols.
Sr John Peter.
Revd John Pridden.
Mr J. R. Syms.
The Chairman informed the above Gentlemen, that he had requested their attendance to impart to them an Idea

FIG. 3. Facsimile of the First Page of the Original Minutes of the Sea-Bathing Hospital (*By permission of the Royal Sea-Bathing Hospital*).

a leader in many charitable and humanitarian organisations. The Aldersgate or General Dispensary treated paupers not only on its own premises but at home, and Lettsom published an account of its work, reprinted in 1775. He conceived the idea of using such dispensaries as medical schools for teaching students clinical medicine. His work in founding the Royal Humane Society, which had its first meeting at the London Coffee House in May 1774, is covered in Chapter III; so also is his achievement in founding the Royal Sea Bathing Hospital at Margate in 1791.

As one of the earliest physicians in London to undertake regular visits to the sick poor in their own homes, Lettsom appreciated the appalling conditions in which many lived and became the only doctor to the debtors' prison in Wood Street (see also "Prisons", Ch. III). Many prisoners were in gaol for debts of only a few pounds and their families were often left destitute; typhus—gaol fever—was almost universal. His daily contact with such conditions, and his realisation of the almost total lack of medical knowledge amongst the apothecaries, inspired him to try and improve the standards of practice. In the 1770s there were few ways of doing this except by arranging meetings, lectures, and opportunities for exchange of information and reading facilities. It was with these objects in mind that Lettsom formed his idea of a Medical Society of London which would break down ignorance and suspicion inside the profession.

His philanthropic activities did not, however, preclude Lettsom from building up a highly successful practice or from becoming a considerable figure in the society of his day. At Sambrook House, Basinghall Street, where he practised until his death in 1815, he earned in perhaps the peak year of his professional life, (1800), the sum of £12,000—equivalent to £100,000 or more today. At that time surgeons earned far less then physicians and the standard fee for major operations was still only about 34p (6/8d.); the average cost of food per patient in hospital was 6d per day. Income tax, first imposed by Pitt in 1799 as a war tax, was then only 10p (2/-) in the £.

FIG. 4a. Lettsom's house at Grove Hill, Camberwell, Surrey.

FIG. 4b. The gardens of Lettsom's house.

Lettsom's day began with seeing perhaps fifty patients, without payment, before breakfast and continued with visits, mainly on foot, to his paying patients, who included many wealthy city merchants. He became very much a fashionable society physician, numbering among his patients Lord Shelborne, first Marquis of Lansdowne, a great patron of the arts and firm opponent of American Independence, and Lord Erskine, Lord Chancellor in 1806 and a strong advocate of Negro Emancipation. Lettsom worked long hours and was rarely able to escape to his country estate at Grove Hill, Camberwell, but he nevertheless made it one of the best-known houses near London. In an area of about 10 acres he cultivated a great variety of rare plants, including over 16 types of grape vines, over 100 fruit trees—apricot, peach, nectarine among them—and shrubs from America, many of them transferred from Fothergill's famous garden at Upton. In one year alone he spent £8,000 on his gardens, and would give elaborate fêtes, entertaining distinguished visitors such as Samuel Johnson and James Boswell, who wrote a Horatian Ode about "Camberwell with Coakley". In it Lettsom is described as:

> West India bred, warm heart, cool head,
> The City's first Physician the name of Dr. Lettsom
> From him of good—talk,
> Liquor, food—his guest will always get some.

An account of an evening's fête at the Grove on May 23rd, 1804, is given in the Gentleman's Magazine, Vol. 74, p. 473.

Despite his fame and wealth, Lettsom, like all consultants of his day, had little ancillary help and had to be both his own nurse and G.P. At the same time, diagnosis was quick, if inaccurate, and little time was spent on investigation, since even the stethoscope had, of course, not yet been discovered. Fig. 5 shows one of Lettsom's accounts, charging less than one guinea for attendance, two guineas for hire of the post-chaise and 2/6 for bleeding. In spite of lampoons about his readiness to treat patients by bleeding, Lettsom was in fact far less ready to adopt this almost universal remedy than were

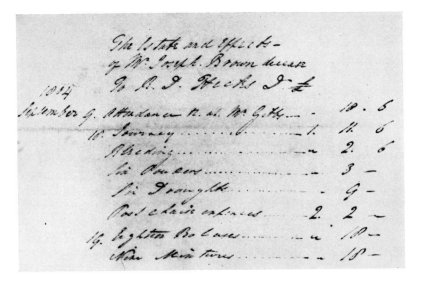

FIG. 5. Lettsom's account for attendance on Mr. Joseph Brown 1804(*Mrs. Martin*).

most other physicians of his day. Indeed, when he heard that his son John had bled himself at the start of a "putrid fever" he became quite distracted and declared that his son "might as well have shot himself".

Lettsom was an early enthusiast for treatment by fresh air and sunlight, and strongly supported the new fashion for sea-bathing, which spread when George III recovered from an attack of insanity after his long visit to Weymouth in 1789. Dr. Richard Russel had written a dissertation in 1753 on the use of sea water in diseases of the glands and sea baths with cold and hot water; sweating and showering baths had been opened at Brighton in 1769 by Dr. Awsiter, who also advised that "sea water mixed with milk made a noble medicine". But it was not until about 1790 that seaside resorts began to compete with the older spas, providing a Master of Ceremonies, Assembly Rooms, and the social amenities of a theatre and parade. The Indian Vapour Bath with massage was introduced by Sake Deen Mahomed at Brighton in 1785, and Sir Astley

Cooper and many fashionable London physicians sent patients there for treatment. The Margate Sea-bathing Hospital is a monument to Lettsom's enthusiasm (see also "Hospitals", Ch. III).

His biographer Clarke contrasts Lettsom with Fothergill who, he says, "practised his profession mainly for the purpose of doing good and made the pecuniary object of his calling the last of his considerations", whereas Lettsom was one of those who "if he spoke of his fee last was the first to think of it". How far this is true is doubtful, but it is quite certain that Lettsom was exceptionally generous with his large fortune as well as lavish in his style of living. He gave generously to charitable causes, such as the Royal Humane Society and the General Dispensary at Aldersgate, as well as to individuals in need. It must have been partly due to these outgoings as well as a decline in his earnings that he was eventually obliged to sell Grove Hill and much of his library. Throughout his life he had collected rare books and manuscripts, most of which were sold. But some he bequeathed to the Medical Society of London, and, as will be seen later in this chapter, he had already presented the freehold of his house in Bolt Court to the Society in 1787. Lettsom died in 1815, his will was proved a year later, and the property was sworn, on April 4th 1822, as worth under £7,000.

His eldest son John Miers went, in the care of Dr. Sims, then president of the Medical Society of London, to Europe in 1792. Two years later he took his M.D. at Leyden, having been a guest, during his tour, of Emma, Lady Hamilton in Naples. Lettsom himself had known her when she was a maid employed by Dr. R. Budd, physician at St. Bartholomew's Hospital. To Lettsom's lasting grief, the son destined to take over his father's practice died of fever at the age of 29—possibly typhus caught during his work at the London Hospital.

One of Lettsom's daughters, Mary Ann, married Philip Elliot and in 1804 her beautiful sister Eliza married his brother John. These marriages were not altogether to Lettsom's liking, for neither son-in-law was a Quaker and John Elliot was also a brewer, a profession not, of course, favoured by Lettsom or

FIG. 6. John Coakley Lettsom with his family in his garden at Grove Hill, Camberwell by a follower of Devis (previously attributed to Zoffany) (*Wellcome Museum*).

the Quakers. He had, indeed, written an account, "Hints respecting the Effects of Hard Drinking (1798)", and a satire against alcohol entitled "The Moral and Physical Thermometer", and although his main objection was to spirits and wine, he had to accept a son-in-law who was virtually the originator of India Pale Ale. But Eliza Elliot was a woman of outstanding beauty and charm, bearing her husband 15 children. They lived at Pimlico Lodge (the Stag Brewery) and were often visited by Lettsom, who, with Dr. Pettigrew (see Ch. IV), took one of his small grandsons from there to Kensington Palace as a vaccination donor to the future Queen Victoria. John Elliot was a patient of Sir Astley Cooper (see Ch. IV), President of the Society in 1826, and died of abdominal tumour in 1829, but his wife survived until 1865, living in the lavish style of her father, with increasing debts and occasional escapes to the continent to avoid her creditors.

The Foundation and brief history of the Medical Society of London

As has been shown earlier in this chapter, Lettsom realised at the start of his career in London that there was an urgent need for a society embracing all departments of the medical profession. The first meeting was held on May 19th 1773, with 15 members, all of them Lettsom's personal friends. By July of that year 29 further members had been elected and in August Dr. John Miller, a physician at the Westminster General Infirmary in Soho, was chosen as President; Lettsom was the first treasurer. At first the society met in different taverns—the Queen's Arms in Newgate Street, the Sun Tavern—but Lettsom had from the start determined to make the Society more than just a friendly group of doctors meeting socially and for discussion. He aimed to develop something permanent and substantial, with its own museum and club premises for members to use. At first numbers were limited to 30 physicians, 30 surgeons and 30 apothecaries, but even so accommodation was a problem. Not until August 1774 did the society finally acquire suitable premises in Crane Court, off Fleet Street, and, after some alterations to provide a large enough meeting room, the Society met there fortnightly until 1788 (see also Ch. VII).

Lettsom read his first paper to the Society, on "The Cause of Pain in Rheumatism", in September 1773, and another on "The Defence of Inoculation" in December. He attended every meeting during the Society's first year of existence. The annual subscription was fixed at one guinea. During 1775 there were serious disagreements among members, and in January the president, Dr. John Millar, locked the door of the room in Crane Court—where the Royal Society was also housed—and an adjourned meeting had to be held in another room. Lettsom was thereupon elected president and the first meeting under his presidency was held on February 28th. Luckily, the alarming quarrels that nearly ended the life of the society were eventually resolved, and a "feast" to celebrate was held at the King's Head

3

tavern on June 16th, at a price of 5/6d per head. After this, meetings continued regularly at Crane Court, although towards the end of Dr. Sims's unbroken presidency of 22 years (see also Ch. IV) membership fell alarmingly.

By 1786 it seemed as if the Society would perish. But Lettsom's determination and generosity gave it a new life; in 1788 he presented No. 3 Bolt Court in Fleet Street to be the permanent home of the society under a trust (see also Ch. VII). There it remained for 62 years, until 1850. At the opening of the premises Lettsom gave an inaugural address. "It must afford peculiar pleasure" he said, "to commence the year under our own roof; to see the number of our associates rapidly multiplied; our library furnished with a collection of valuable books; our table covered with donations; and our meetings honoured with communications from the professors of our art not only in Europe but from the Indies and America." Referring to the stone plaque over the door of the new house—now preserved in the lecture room at Chandos Street—he memorably and vehemently voiced his condemnation of quacks and his lifelong fight against dishonest practice; he compared the "depredation and mischief", represented in the carving by Isis and two Theban sphinxes, to "every bold and ignorant empiric"; "Let us", he exorted his audience, "as a phalanx of medical strength, attempt to break the spell of dark mystery, secret nostrums and poisonous arcana, and place the practice of our art upon the liberal and enlarged system of true science and medical experience."

Bolt Court had been left to the society so long as the number of fellows did not fall below twenty for six months. If this ever occurred, the house was to become the property of his legal representative. By 1850 membership of the society had fallen to about 60, mainly due to the gradual decline of the City as a social and residential area. At the same time another society— was finding difficulty in keeping up its numbers. This society had been founded in 1809 by Sir C. Mansfield Clarke and Sir Benjamin Brodie and had for many years met at the School of Medicine in Great Windmill Street, boasting over 1,000

members, mainly students attending the school. When the
school broke up, the society met for a time at 32 Sackville
Street, and later in Savile Row, but by 1850 there were only
237 names on its list. The presidents of the two societies, Mr.
Hird (Westminster) and Dr. Risdon Russell (Medical Society
of London) (see also Ch. IV), showed remarkable cooperation
and readiness to amalgamate. By 1851, the year of the Great
Exhibition, the two societies had merged under the title of the
Medical Society of London and had taken a twenty-one year
lease of premises at 32 George Street, Hanover Square. Dr.

Fig. 7. The figure of Isis on the plaque which was above the door of the Society's
house in Bolt Court, 1788.

Murphy and Dr. Herd, the two presidents of the Westminster Medical Society concerned (1849 and 1850) must have been magnanimous and liberal men to give up the old name of Westminster and lose the individuality of a society which really dated back to the Lyceum Medicum Londinense of 1785, founded under the patronage of John Hunter and Dr. Fordyce.

This amalgamation with the Westminster Society finally settled the decision of the Medical Society of London to leave the City and move west to the Marylebone area, now becoming both fashionable and the main centre of medical practice. John Coakley Elliott, Lettsom's grandson and the same who had acted as vaccination donor to the Princess Victoria, was heir-at-law and a Trustee of Bolt Court. He was by now a man of substance in the big firm of Elliot Watney, Brewers and, as Clarke writes, "in the handsomest manner he resigned all interest in the house which became the property of the Society and was then let at a very inadequate rent" (see also Ch. VII).

Marylebone was, by 1850, very different from the days of Lettsom and the early years of the Medical Society of London. At that time the old Marylebone Gardens, which had been patronised by Pepys and Dr. Johnson, were converted into the Marylebone Spa, covering several acres where Beaumont, Devonshire, and Weymouth Streets now cross. The Spa, whose medicinal waters were reputed to improve digestion, closed in 1778 and residential buildings soon began to appear. Though Cavendish Square had been built about 1715, Harley Street was still called "Harley Fields" and was described as "a dreary and monotonous waste between Cavendish Square and Marylebone Village", the first houses in Harley Street not appearing before about 1752.

But, in less than a century, a large and socially aristocratic district had materialised; by 1823 Matthew Baillie, Physician to George III, was living in Cavendish Square at No. 25, and by 1850 R. Quain and others had come to the district, making it a centre of consultant practice.

The now revitalised Medical Society of London held regular meetings in its new premises in George Street until the expiration of the 21-year lease. The year before its centenary, 1872, a special meeting was held at which the society approved its council's recommendation to acquire new premises at No. 11 Chandos Street. Again a 21-year lease was proposed, and it was agreed that £500 to £600 would be needed to alter the building so as to "enable the Society to enlarge its borders, if desirable to accommodate sister societies, and by arrangement with a bookseller to provide accommodation so as to utilise its valuable library" (see also Chs. V and VII). Although some members complained that they "did not like leaving the old nest", the decision to move was taken.

A centenary celebration dinner was held on March 8th 1873 at Willis's Room, King Street, St. James's, at which there were 80 stewards. The price was 21/- per head. The President in 1792, Thomas Bryant F.R.C.S., congratulated the society on its acquisition of new premises which, though unfurnished, gave, he said, "promise of being equal to all the requirements of the Society". He referred to such great advances as the microscope and the clinical thermometer and emphasised that the Society invited contributions from every branch of science.

The new premises had distinguished neighbours and must have been regarded as highly fashionable. The new Langham Hotel, first of the "monster" hotels in London, with a staff of over 250 and a lift which went up and down from time to time, had replaced Foley House in 1862. No. 11 was owned by Charles George, Earl of Gainsborough (b.1818) who married Adelaide Harriet Augusta, illegitimate daughter of the Duke of Clarence (later William IV). The Earl died in a hansom cab in the Tottenham Court Road in 1881, but his wife lived on for some years and is described as having been "exceedingly handsome and like the rest of her family of stern and unbending piety". Their residence was 9 Cavendish Square and for many years No. 11 was occupied by Sir Gerard Noel Bt. whose home was Exton Park, Stamford. Chandos House was the home of Prince Esterhazy, the Austrian Ambassador; the Rt. Hon.

Joseph Planta M.P. had lived for many years at No. 10—he was Keeper of Manuscripts and Chief Librarian at the British Museum, an office the duties of which, it is said, "he discharged by deputy whilst mixing in political and official circles"; at No. 5 lived Miss Warren and the Ladies Grenville.

When the Medical Society moved into No. 11 considerable changes were made. The front was altered to provide additional entrances, the present doorway to No. 10A being then the main entrance to No. 11. In 1876 the building was shared with the Royal Historical Society and in 1883 a mortgage was taken out in the sum of £4,000 from the Briton Life Assurance Society in order to acquire the freeholds of Nos. 11 and 12 (see also Ch. VII).

But Bolt Court, its donor and the Society's Founder, are not forgotten by those who meet in Chandos Street today. "The Medical Society of London" writes Abraham, "is Lettsom's Monument: practically all the investigations he did, the papers he produced, were presented before it. He lives in its archives and its history, for the first forty years of its existence is his history". The influence of his wide interests in different fields of knowledge will be seen in the list of remarkable presidents and orations delivered since the Society's foundation which are detailed in Chapter IV.

Some Sources of Information Referred to in Chapter I

The author is indebted to Johnston Abraham's excellent study: Lettsom, His Life, times, friends and descendants (Heinemann, 1933), now hard to find, but available in the Society's Library. Also the following sources are acknowledged:

Fordyce, Sir William (1773) A New Enquiry into the Causes of Fevers.
Farrer, W. (1773) A Particular Account of the Rickets in Children.
Clarke, J. F. (1874) Autobiographical Recollections of the Medical Profession London. J. & A. Churchill.
Gentlemen's Magazine (1788) LVIII. 97 and 98.
Thomson, Sir St. Clair. (1918) John Coakley Lettsom. London. Harrison & Son.
Dukes, Cuthbert E., O.B.E. (1960) London Medical Societies in the Eighteenth Century. Proc. Roy. Soc. Med., LIII, 699–706.
Bailey, J. B. (1895) Medical Institutions of London. B.M.J. II, 26.
Old and New London. Cassell & Co. Vol. IV.

Janes, Hurford (1963) The Red Barrel. (A History of Watney Mann). John Murray.

Bryan, C. P. (1932) Roundabout Harley Street. London. John Bale.

Armour, Donald, C. M. G. (1929) Some of Lettsom's Contemporaries. *Lancet*, **ii**, 855.

Annotation (1955) The Story of the R.S.M. *Lancet*, **i**, 1209.

Abraham, J. Johnston (1943–46) The Two Fothergills. Trans: *Med. Soc. Lond.* LXIV, 276–291.

Chapter II

The Medley Painting

SIR ERIC RICHES

The Medical Society of London is fortunate in the possession of a portrait of some of its leading members in the years succeeding its foundation. We owe it to the much maligned James Sims, who was at least sincere in his loyalty to the society, that the portrait was painted at all. Sims had rendered a professional service to Medley the artist and in return and in lieu of fee, Medley agreed to paint a portrait of Sims (Fig. 1). It was considered so successful that the same artist was commissioned to paint the group which is the subject of this chapter.

The Artist

Samuel Medley was born in Liverpool in 1769; he was the son of a well-known Baptist minister who enjoyed the reputation of being a good preacher. He appears to have come to London at the age of 21, as he was a student at the Royal Academy Schools on October 14th 1791. He had a studio at 13, Tavistock Row and in 1792 his first exhibit, "The Last Supper", was shown at the Royal Academy. Moving to 5, Golden Square in 1793 he completed seven more pictures, principally of historical, classical and religious scenes, all of which were exhibited. In 1797 he was at 98 Leadenhall Street and here he concentrated on portraits. He was a follower of Reynolds and Gainsborough and excelled in "photographic" portraits. By 1798 he had moved to his final studio at 52,

22

Threadneedle Street and from here until 1805 he produced sixteen paintings, mainly portraits, for exhibition. The portrait of James Sims was exhibited in 1798, during the twelfth year of his presidency. The commission for the large group picture followed but this was never shown at the Royal Academy.

The group portrait is often known as "The Founders Picture". It contains however only four of the original Founder Fellows, Lettsom, Nathaniel Hulme, Edward Ford and Charles Combe, and was probably painted in 1800, twenty-eight years after our foundation. It may have been composed to commemorate Lettsom's presentation of the title deeds of No. 3, Bolt Court to the Society in 1788, twelve years earlier.

The inscription on the engraving, done by Nathan Branwhite in 1801, has the caption "The President, Fellows and Corresponding Members of the Medical Society of London. This print of the principal institutors is inscribed by their obliged humble servant Samuel Medley". There is no date. There are only two corresponding members, John Shadwell and Edward Jenner, who was elected in 1803 and whose portrait was added later. Johnston Abraham (1933) suggests that it represents a series of accurate portraits of the chief personages in the Medical Society of London around 1800. Clutterbuck, one of the most influential members of the Society who knew all the men shown in the picture, said that "Nothing could be more lifelike". It would seem likely that each individual was studied and painted separately so as to be easily recognisable in the group as is the practice of many modern artists.

Medley had other medical men as his sitters; there is an excellent portrait in the Royal College of Surgeons of Joseph Warner who was Master of the Company in 1780 and in 1784. It was painted by Medley in 1801 not long before Warner's death at the age of 84. Warner was born at Antigua in the same group of West Indian islands as Lettsom; Medley may have known him through Lettsom as he already knew Sims, Babington, Blair, Hooper and Jenner.

Medley's eldest daughter Susannah was the mother of Sir Henry Thompson of University College Hospital, born in 1820.

Thompson inherited some of his grandfather's talent and was himself no mean artist; he exhibited at the Royal Academy and at the Paris Salon and had a valuable collection of Chinese porcelain. He was extremely versatile; he wrote two successful novels under the pseudonym of "Pen Oliver, F.R.C.S."; one, "All But, a Chronicle of Laxenford" contains a self-portrait drawn in 1885.

Medley continued to work at Threadneedle Street and to exhibit at the Royal Academy. He attained a much greater power with the brush, as several of his pictures in Thompson's possession show, but the confinement to a studio in London air injured his health so severely that his medical friends advised him to relinquish art as a profession; he did so at the age of 36. Instead he took to the Stock Exchange where he made a large fortune, or, as Thompson described it, "a comfortable competency" (Clarke 1874). He retired to an active social and literary life. He was foremost in agitating for a free non-

Fig. 8a. The Founders' Picture by Samuel Medley, 1800.

sectarian education for all and was one of the founders of University College London, a non-sectarian institution; as a proprietor he nominated Thompson as a student there. He spent the latter part of his life at Chatham where he died on August 10th 1857 at the age of 88—having outlived the medical warning by over 50 years.

The Picture

There are twenty-two persons, wearing the wigs and dress of the period, shown grouped at a table. Most are in dark clothes with white cravats and knee-breeches with light stockings; Sir John Hayes (2) and Dr. John Relph (21) are dressed in a lighter brown material and Edward Jenner (11) is in grey. All the wigs are powdered except that of Dr. John Aitken (17).

Fig. 8b. The Key to the Picture.

1. Dr. John Coakley Lettsom. 2. Sir John Hayes. 3. Dr. James Sims. 4. Dr. Thomas Bradley. 5. Dr. James Ware. 6. Dr. Edward Bancroft. 7. Dr. Joseph Hart Myers (*Librarian*). 8. Mr. William Woodville. 9. Dr. Nathaniel Hulme. 10. Dr. Sayer Walker. 11. Dr. Edward Jenner. 12. Dr. Robert Hooper (*Secretary*). 13. Mr. Edward Ford. 14. Dr. John Heighton. 15. Dr. Robert John Thornton. 16. Mr. John Shadwell. 17. Dr. John Aikin. 18. Mr. William Blair. 19. Dr. William-Babington. 20. Dr. Charles Combe. 21. Dr. John Relph. 22. Dr. William Saunders.

The faces are for the most part serious although there is more than a hint of a smile on that of James Sims (3). The general sombreness of the colouring is relieved by the red patterned tablecloth.

In the background are three busts; the one on the right is alleged to represent Hewson, that on the left appears to be Dr. Smith, and that in the centre Deane. They are not present in the engraving. Originally there were twenty-one members but Edward Jenner was added after the picture had been painted and engraved. He became a corresponding member in about 1790 and was elected an ordinary Fellow in 1802. In the following year he was awarded the Fothergillian Medal; this was the last of the John Fothergill medals. The portrait of Jenner was added by Medley on instruction but before this the picture had been engraved by Nathan Branwhite and a few copies had been struck. Branwhite cut a hole in the plate and inserted a new square of copper on which he engraved the head, which explains why it is somewhat smaller than the others and out of perspective. There are said to be a few copies of the engraving without the head of Jenner but the Society does not possess one.

The grouping of the figures has been faulted by some critics but Thompson pointed out that it had to be altered to meet the tastes and sense of propriety of the members; even if it is not altogether what the artist wished the subjects are so arranged that their faces are recognisable and the likenesses are excellent.

The picture was cleaned and revarnished in 1854 and in 1970 was again cleaned at the National Gallery, and hung over the mantelpiece in the newly-decorated Fellows Room where its colours and detail can be seen to full advantage.

It has been described previously, with annotations on the members, notably by St. Clair Thomson in 1917 (published 1918) and by Tanner (1947). The account given by Dr. E. Symes Thompson in his Annual Oration in 1882 does not appear to have been published. The numbered key to the individuals is the one adopted by St. Clair Thomson; the individuals concerned are listed in Table I.

Brief biographical details are given about those Fellows who are not described in other chapters . . .

1. *Dr. John Coakley Lettsom* (1744–1815)
   See previous chapter.

2. *Sir John M'Namara Hayes* (1750–1809)
   The courtier physician, elegant and handsome. He wears a brown suit with light stockings. He was born in Limerick and graduated at Rheims, entered the army and became physician to the Forces in 1784. In 1791 he was appointed Physician Extraordinary to the Prince of Wales and a year later physician to Westminster Hospital. His success in the Havannah campaign led to a baronetcy in 1797. At the time of his death from acute laryngitis in 1809 he was Inspector-General of the Medical Department in the Ordnance. There is a tablet to his memory in St. James' Church, Piccadilly.

3. *Dr. James Sims* (1741–1820)
   President from 1786 to 1808, the first Orator in 1774 (see Ch. IV). His portrait is a replica of the one painted by Medley two years earlier save that he is wearing the Presidential cocked hat, in accordance with Lettsom's rule that "the President whilst in the Chair shall be covered, except when addressing himself to the whole Society".

4. *Dr. Thomas Bradley* (1751–1813)
   Orator 1800. He was deaf and is shown with his hand cupping his left ear. He taught mathematics before taking up medicine. His appointment as physician to Westminster Hospital in 1794 in succession to Sir John Hayes provided a great contrast in personalities. As co-editor of the Medical and Physical Journal Bradley was involved in an action for damages by Brodum, a medical quack who had been attacked in the Journal for his remedies. Lettsom, who was responsible for the article, had to pay £390 to settle the affair.

5. Mr. *James Ware, F.R.S.* (1756–1815)

Orator 1797. He was the most distinguished ophthalmic surgeon of his time and had a reputation as an unusually deft cataract extractor. He wrote extensively on his own subject and also on urological topics. He is credited with being the first to recognise the true nature of ophthalmia neonatorum, and he also noted the gonorrhoeal origin of the purulent ophthalmia in soldiers returned from Egypt. He was a founder of the school for the Indigent Blind, and of the Society for the Relief of Widows and Orphans of Medical men, of which he later became president. He raised ophthalmology from being near to quackery to becoming a proper branch of medicine. His great-great-grandson is Editor of the British Medical Journal, and *his* elder son is also in the medical profession.

Ware is recognisable in the picture as the only one wearing spectacles.

6. Dr. *Edward Bartholomew Bancroft, F.R.S.* (1744–1821)

One of the two Americans in the picture and one who attained notoriety by his show of allegiance to each side during the American War of Independence. He was born at Westfield Massachusetts of a good New England family, ran away to sea as a boy but returned in time to repay what he owed. His career has been fully described by MacNalty (1944).

He was certainly industrious and in early life acquired a knowledge of chemistry and botany and their use in dye production. Coming to England in 1765 or 1766, he became a medical student, probably at St. Bartholomew's Hospital, but later obtained an M.D. of Aberdeen. He wrote extensively, including a novel as well as scientific papers. He was elected F.R.S. for his papers on Communicating Colours. He was a friend of Lettsom and acted as secretary for the meeting of the Medical Society at which Lettsom became President. In 1775 he obtained a government patent for the yellow oak bark which he named quercitron; this was his personal discovery and it ensured him a good income although he was always short of money.

He appeared and behaved as a patriotic American and suggested a means of settlement of the War of Independence but Paul Wentowrth, an American agent of the British Intelligence Service, induced him to act as double spy. He received instructions from Benjamin Franklin, disclosed secret negotiations with the French to the British and accepted payment from both sides. He speculated on the Stock Exchange, shipped contraband to America and passed on information about English politics to Deane, the first diplomatic representative of the United States in Paris. He held up information about Burgoyne's surrender at Saratoga in order to make a large profit on the Stock Exchange.

His monopoly of the sale of quercitron was not renewed but his salary as a British agent was increased from £500 to £1,000.

After the war he continued his valuable work on dye production, the first important research on the subject in the English language, and was never found out as a spy until 70 years after his death.

7. *Dr. Joseph Hart-Myers* (1758–1823)

The other American in the picture, who was born in New York; his parents were Jewish. As a young man he came to London and attended the lectures of William Hunter, and of George Fordyce. He later went to Edinburgh where he obtained his M.D. in 1778. Returning to London he became physician to the Portugese Hospital and a colleague of Lettsom on the staff of the Aldersgate Street General Dispensary. He was Librarian to the Society.

8. *Dr. William Woodville, F.R.S.* (1752–1805)

A Quaker and a friend of Lettsom, was born at Cockermouth in Cumberland and practised in that county after gaining his M.D. at Edinburgh in 1775. In London in 1784 he was elected Physician to the Smallpox and Inoculation Hospitals. He was a skilled botanist, established a large garden in the grounds of the Smallpox Hospital at King's Cross, and produced a magnificent work in four volumes on medical botany.

Having been involved in the inoculation controversy in the 1770s, he was at first sceptical about vaccination and opposed it, but met Jenner at the Medical Society and after discussion and friendly argument became a staunch supporter of vaccination. He organised a clinical trial which was so successful as to give confidence to his potential patients.

He died of dropsy in March 1805 and was buried in the Friends' burial ground.

He is shown in the picture seated with his legs crossed behind Sir John Hayes.

9. Dr. Nathaniel Hulme, F.R.S. (1732–1807)

A Founder, President in 1776 and Orator in 1777. In the picture he sits on the left between Woodville and Sayer Walker. (see also Ch. IV).

10. Dr. Sayer Walker (1748–1826)

An obstetrician and psychiatrist and colleague of Lettsom at the City of London Lying-in Hospital. Born at Bocking in Essex. Spencer Paterson (1968 and 1971) has produced evidence that he was the unknown English friend of Pinel referred to by Semelaigne, the French historian. Walker subsequently became Pastor of the Presbyterian Church at Enfield, attended a course of lectures by Dr. William Saunders of Guy's Hospital (No. 22 in the picture) also a Presbyterian, and became deeply interested in psychological medicine. He has been called the Father of psychosomatic psychiatry in England. It is on this, rather than his successful use of turpentine in 90 cases of Taenia, that his reputation will rest.

11. Dr. Edward Jenner (1749–1823)

Jenner had been accepted as a corresponding member of the Society in 1790 and was elected an ordinary Fellow in 1802. He was awarded the Fothergillian medal in 1803 and it was felt that a fellow of such distinction should be incorporated in the painting (see also "Vaccination" Ch. III).

12. *Dr. Robert Hooper* (1773–1857)

An M.D. of St. Andrew's who practised in Savile Row, and was secretary at the time the picture was painted. He sits in the middle of the table holding a quill pen.

This is not the Joseph Hooper who gave the Oration in 1787; it was Robert who produced a Medical Directory.

13. *Mr. Edward Ford* (1746–1809)

A Founder, secretary for many years, and Orator in 1799. A surgeon who lived at Mark Lane; he was a staunch supporter of the Medical Society and of the establishment. He aided Dr. Millar, the first President, who had quarrelled with Sims, in excluding the Fellows from the Society's House on January 18th 1775 by keeping the keys.

Ford spoke and wrote on the use of electricity in the treatment of headache and of aphonia. He also wrote on diseases of the hip joint. He sits next to Dr. Hooper who took up his method of treating loss of voice.

14. *Dr. John Haighton* (1755–1823)

A very able Guy's physician who was a skilled anatomist, physiologist and obstetrician. So great was his reputation as the ablest teacher of midwifery in Europe that he gave the lectures on diseases of the uterus in Cline's course. Prosecuted by the Royal College of Physicians for practising without a licence, he offered to sit the examination and pay the fee but refused to live for two years at a university and attend lectures given by men who were his inferior. He was a kind and generous man with a great regard for truth, but inclined to be irritable as he had a chronic cough.

15. *Dr. Robert John Thornton* (1768–1837)

He sits on the right of the picture between Haighton and Shadwell. He lectured at Guy's Hospital on medical botany, a subject to which much greater importance was then attached. His work "The British Flora" did not sell well at first but is now much sought after. He was a supporter of Jenner and wrote "A Vindication of Small-pox" as well as a major work entitled "Philosophy of Medicine". We have the 4th Edition (1799) of the five volumes of this work in the Library. It is dedicated "From the author, as a small Tribute of his respect for the Bolt Court Medical Society, by a Friend to Improvements".

16. *Mr. John Shadwell* (fl. 1790)

He practised at Brentwood in Essex. In 1790 he read a paper to the Society on the internal and external use of oil in the treatment of hydrophobia. For this he was awarded a silver medal and elected a Corresponding Member (Memoirs Vol. 3).

17. *Dr. John Aikin* (1747–1822)

A Dissenter, described by Lettsom as a militant Unitarian. He was the biographer of John Howard and supported him in all his work towards reform of conditions in prisons. Aikin's elder son Charles was appointed the first Secretary of the Medico-Chirurgical Society on 28th June 1805; his younger son John was lecturer in chemistry at Guy's Hospital. In the picture his wig is unpowdered, if indeed he is wearing one.

18. *Mr. William Blair* (1766–1822)

Surgeon to the Lock Hospital and to the Finsbury and Bloomsbury Dispensaries. He contended that the honour of being President of the Medical Society should not be restricted to physicians but that a surgeon should be chosen. When Dr. Pinckard was due to retire as President on March 8th 1813 the surgeons were anxious that either Taunton or Blair should succeed him, although the social status of a surgeon in those days was still humble. Taunton was an unlettered man but a zealous anatomist; he was not considered suitable. Blair, on the other hand, was a scholar and a gentleman, but an overbearing person, definitely unpopular. Neither side would accept the other's nominee. Eventually they did the wise thing and asked Lettsom to take office for the third time. Blair was disappointed; he tried to get Lettsom to agree to a surgeon being appointed as the next President. In the event the old conservative attitude was maintained and no surgeon was elected President until Thomas Callaway in 1829 (see also Ch. III). Peace was preserved and the way was cleared for the institution of the present system in which a physician and a surgeon alternate; from time to time a general practitioner or a pathologist or other specialist takes a turn.

19. *Dr. William Babington, F.R.S.* (1756–1833)

Born in Ireland, a tall, powerful man, and a founder with Lettsom of the Athletac, a "keep fit" club restricted to twelve medical men. He was prominent not only in our society but also in the Hunterian Society and was the acknowledged head of the profession in the City. He was apothecary and later physician to Guy's Hospital and looked after Lettsom in his last illness (see also Ch. III).

20. *Dr. Charles Combe, F.R.S.* (1743–1817)

Although one of the Founder members on May 19th 1773 he never became President or Orator. He was a friend and executor of William Hunter and successor in his practice, and like Hunter, a skilled numismatist; he prepared the first volume of the catalogue of Hunter's collection of coins. He was appointed obstetrician to the British Lying-in Hospital in 1789. He was a scholar of distinction and collaborated in a two volume translation of Horace, said to contain the best index which has ever appeared. A life-long friend of Lettsom, whom he proposed for election to the Society of Antiquaries of London, a doubtful honour at the time as the Society was under much criticism.

21. *Dr. John Relph* (1750–1804)

President and Orator 1785. A physician at Guy's Hospital. He was described as a quiet little man without much personality.

He followed the expelled Whitehead in the Presidential chair and was involved in the James Sims controversy. His medical interest was in the Red Peruvian bark which yeilded $1\frac{1}{2}\%$ to 4% of quinine. The powdered bark was very astringent but its preparations were useful until quinine was separated from the other alkaloids.

22. Dr. William Saunders, F.R.S. (1743–1817)

Physician to Guy's Hospital. He sits behind Lettsom, next to Relph. He was industrious, successful in practice, and a good lecturer. In March 1805 he resigned his seat on the Council of the Society in protest against James Sims' retention of the Presidency. Saunders led the secession group which founded the Medical and Chirurgical Society in May 1805; one of their first rules was "That no gentlemen shall be eligible to the Office of President or Vice-President for more than two years in succession". This remains the custom of the Royal Society of Medicine, its successor.

TABLE I
The Key to the Picture

1. Dr. John Coakley Lettsom.
2. Sir John Hayes.
3. Dr. James Sims.
4. Dr. Thomas Bradley.
5. Mr. James Ware.
6. Dr. Edward Bancroft.
7. Dr. Joseph Hart Myers (Librarian).
8. Dr. William Woodville.
9. Dr. Nathaniel Hulme.
10. Dr. Sayer Walker.
11. Dr. Edward Jenner.
12. Dr. Robert Hooper (Secretary).
13. Mr. Edward Ford.
14. Dr. John Heighton.
15. Dr. Robert John Thornton.
16. Mr. John Shadwell.
17. Dr. John Aikin.
18. Mr. William Blair.
19. Dr. William Babington.
20. Dr. Charles Combe.
21. Dr. John Relph.
22. Dr. William Saunders.

Works Consulted

Abraham, J. Johnston (1933) Lettsom, His life, times, friends and descendants. Heinemann, London.

Armour, D. (1930) *Trans. Med. Soc. Lond.* **53,** 3.

Bryan (1904) Dictionary of Painters and Engravers 3, 313. Bell, London.

Clarke, J. F. (1874) Autobiographical Recollections of the Medical Profession (Letter from Sir Henry Thompson), p. 242. Churchill, London.

Cope, Z. (1950) *Brit. J. Urol.* **22,** 3.

Davidson, M. (1955) The Royal Society of Medicine. R.S.M., London.

Dictionary of National Biography (1894) Ed. S. Lee. **37,** 206. Smith, Elder, London.

Dukes, C. E. (1960) *Proc. Roy. Soc. Med.,* **53,** 699.

Graves Dictionary, The Royal Academy exhibitors, p. 225.

Illingworth, C. (1967) The Story of William Hunter. Livingstone, Edinburgh and London.

MacNalty, A. (1944) *Proc. Roy. Soc. Med.* **38,** 7.

Paterson, A. Spencer (1968) Cong. Psych. Neuro de langue française 66th Session Clairmont Ferrand Sept, 1968. Comptes rendus pp. 405, 410.

Paterson, A. Spencer (1971) *Proc. R. Soc. Med.* (Section History of Med.) In the Press.

Power, d'Arcy (1917) *Trans. Med. Soc. Lond.* **40,** 1.

Power, d'Arcy (1920) *Idem.* **43,** 253.

Power, d'Arcy (1931) *Brit. J. Surg.* **19,** 1.

Tanner, W. E. (1947) *Trans. Med. Soc. Lond.* **65,** 226–348.

Thomson, St. Clair. (1918) *Trans. Med. Soc. Lond.* **41,** 1.

Chapter III

The Society's Influence on Medicine and the Community

Ewart M. Jepson

In 1773 the Medical Society of London was founded in a lull between the storms in Europe, and during its first forty years of existence there was unrest within the Society, and wars without. The British were demoralised in the early eighteenth century—this had been a slow process following the Restoration, and Sir Robert Walpole did little to inspire confidence. There was much corruption, crime and destitution and relief was sought in cheap and powerful gin. In Europe Frederick the Great opened the campaigns of the Seven Years War and England had little influence in politics.

Then there was a dramatic change in our military standing, when Clive won India by the victory of Plassey in 1757. In Europe the turning-point came with the successes at Minden and Quiberon Bay 1759, while Wolfe won Quebec in the same year, thereby bringing Canada, and with it America, into the British Empire. In 1763 the Peace of Paris brought the Seven Years War to an end. In 1768 Captain Cook added Australia and New Zealand to the Empire. England had by now acquired tremendous prestige, within twelve years she had become the most powerful country in the world.

But Pitt's disagreement with King George III disrupted internal peace, the American colonies were discontented, and apprehension was spreading. At this moment, in 1773, our

Society was founded by Lettsom. War broke out with America in 1775, France and Spain joined America, and England capitulated and accepted the 1776 Declaration of Independence in 1782. Europe soon erupted in the French Revolution (1789) and the ensuing war with France led to privation and distress which dragged on until 1815. There is no doubt that the French Revolution brought the pre-eminence of French medicine to an end and the opportunity passed to England where the Medical Society of London was at its heart.

America

There is no greater honour to our Society than the part it played in the development of American medicine. Lettsom himself held sixteen American honours, and amongst 56 signatories of the Declaration of Independence in 1776 there were six physicians. They were Benjamin Rush, a Fellow of the Society, Joseph Bartlett, Leiman Hall, George Taylor, Matthew Thornton and Oliver Wolcott.

Benjamin Franklin, a Quaker, who was a corresponding member of the Medical Society of London by 1789, was an

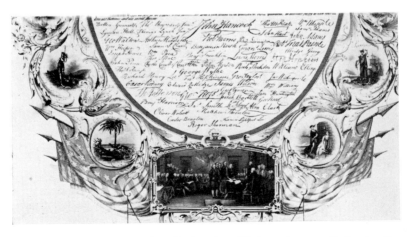

Fig. 9. A section of the American Declaration of Independence 1776, showing the signatures of Benjamin Rush, Joseph Bartlett, Leiman Hall, George Taylor, Matthew Thornton and Oliver Wolcott (*British Museum*).

agent of the American colonies, living in Paris from 1776 onwards. The Quaker colony in Pennsylvania had close links with their brethren in England, and in London with the great physicians Fothergill and Lettsom, both of whom were friends of Franklin. There is in the library of the Society a tract "Some account of the Pennsylvania Hospital" and among the managers of the hospital in 1753 are the names of Benjamin Franklin and Evan Morgan—the latter was the father of John Morgan, founder of American medicine.

John Morgan trained in London and attended William Hewson's and William Hunter's lectures in the Great Windmill Street school. He then went to Edinburgh, where William Cullen taught in English, not the usual Latin, and gained his M.D. in 1763. He obtained the licence from the Royal College of Physicians in 1765, returned to America and worked for the establishment of schools of medicine. In 1769 he witnessed the first fruits of his labour in Philadelphia when several gentlemen received the first American medical academic honours. John Morgan became director-general and physician-in-chief to the general hospital of the American Army in 1775. He survived a libel action and died in 1789, and was succeeded by Dr. Benjamin Rush, the friend of Lettsom.

Benjamin Rush was one of the signatories of the Declaration of Independence. He was made a corresponding member of the Medical Society of London in 1784 and given the honour at a meeting in 1813 of having his contributions to medicine commemorated. He was a protégé of Benjamin Franklin, who supported his medical education in Europe after he graduated from Princeton at the precocious age of 15. He took his Edinburgh M.D. aged 23. When he returned to America in 1769 he was appointed to the staff of the Pennsylvania Hospital, becoming Professor of Medicine in 1797. He and Lettsom had met at Fothergill's house and struck up a friendship which was to continue throughout their lives, despite the War of Independence. Even during those troubled times Lettsom was deputed by the Society to send books to the Library of the Pennsylvania Hospital, and acted as agent in commissioning an engraving of the hospital which they wished to have made in London.

Rush was a man of very fixed ideas, and a difficult colleague. It was in the great epidemic of yellow fever in 1793 that he provoked the greatest opposition. He concluded that yellow fever was indigenous to America and non-contagious. In this he ran counter to all the public and professional opinions of his time. He advocated the "Two-ten treatment", purging with 10 grains each of calomel and jalap, followed by bleeding to faintness. Time and again he wrote to Lettsom asserting his theories on yellow fever but evidently Lettsom did not agree with him, and their disagreement lasted until Rush died in 1813. Rush owned some land on Sugar Creek in America, one portion of which he called Lettsom and the other Fothergill. Two American friends of Lettsom, Dr. D. Hosack and Dr. Samuel L. Mitchell, both opposed Rush's views and wrote to Lettsom accordingly.

Dr. Hosack first used the stethoscope in America and is also remembered for his Elgin Botanical Garden in New York which cost him $100,000. He could not keep it up, selling to the city of New York for $80,000. In 1814 Columbia University took it over and it is probably now the most valuable site for its size in the world as on part of it stand Fifth Avenue and Radio City.

Another famous American, Dr. Benjamin Waterhouse, was a cousin of Fothergill, living with him during his medical training, and then striking up a friendship with Lettsom which lasted until his death. Waterhouse returned to America after the war ended in 1781 and was appointed Professor of the Theory and Practice of Medicine at the newly-founded Harvard Medical School at Cambridge, seven miles from Boston, in 1872. Waterhouse was a cantankerous man, much better educated than any of the other academics in Boston, which seems to have given him a feeling of superiority resented by his colleagues. Lettsom, who corresponded regularly with Waterhouse, made Harvard a gift of 700 specimens of European minerals and was henceforth known as the father of the science of mineralogy in America.

It was Waterhouse who received details of Jenner's vaccination theory from Lettsom and it was to him that supplies of vaccine were sent (see p. 46). He retired in 1812 but lived on to 92, dying in 1846.

A less well known friend of Lettsom was Nathan Smith. He founded four medical schools in America at Dartmouth College, Yale, Bowdoin and Vermont. He was one of the earliest medical graduates from Harvard and came to London in 1796 armed with his own enthusiasm and borrowed money to get books and instruments, generously helped by Lettsom. When he returned to America Smith had a hard struggle but eventually succeeded, being offered the Chair of Medicine and Surgery at Yale when it was established in 1812.

Dr. William Thornton (1761–1828) designed the Capitol building in Washington. He was a Quaker also from Tortola Lettsom's birthplace, a friend of Lettsom and corresponding member of the Medical Society of London. He graduated at Edinburgh and went to Philadelphia where he complained he had difficulty in finding a wife to suit his requirements. While there his interest in architecture was such that his plan for a new building of a Philadelphia library, founded by Benjamin Franklin, was accepted. He returned to practise in Tortola and heard of the competition to plan the Capitol and President's house in Washington. He prepared his plans and sailed for Philadelphia, but arrived too late for the competition. None of the 14 plans submitted was satisfactory, so Thornton approached George Washington directly; the President was delighted with the "grandeur, simplicity and convenience" and the Secretary of State, Thomas Jefferson, was also impressed with the "simple, noble, beautiful and excellently arranged" plan. It is today the most famous building in America. Following this Thornton received public office and abandoned his Quaker upbringing, joining the Militia and fighting in 1812; he lost his earlier zeal for the abolition of slavery. He remained a close friend of George Washington, writing frequently to Lettsom about him. He describes a dinner party given by George Washington who complained that a fire behind him was too large and hot. "A gentleman observed it behoved the General to stand fire. 'Yes', said Washington, 'but it does not look well for a General to receive the fire behind'."

The story of the double spy, Dr. Edward Bancroft, an American and famous Fellow of the Society, is given in Chapter II.

Prisons

In eighteenth century England the penal code was extremely harsh and prison conditions appalling. Debtors were thrown into gaol for comparatively minor offences and expected to remain there often alongside common felons. If they could prove they had no money the creditor had to pay for their "groats", about 4d a day, but such help was rarely obtained for the debtor had no means of going to law to enforce payment.

The prison governor made his living from the fees due on admission and discharge and was open to corruption of every kind. The prisoners earned money to pay for their food by carrying on their trade; if this was impracticable, they risked starvation. No clothing was supplied at all. In this miserable state the prisoners spent their earnings largely on gin and beer which were cheap. Often there was no surgeon or apothecary and no hospital for them if they were ill. The General Dispensary in Aldersgate Street was close to a debtors' gaol, known as the Wood Street Compter. Lettsom was physician to the dispensary, found that the gaol had no physician, and offered his services. He describes the state of prisoners who were verminous and slept on shelves with no bedding and practically no sanitation, the whole pervading a vile smell. He mentions many deaths from typhus and notes that the gaol fever was spread in the crowded courtyards of the city by discharged prisoners. The eminent and rich were not immune and in the famous incident of the Black Assize of 1750 the Lord Mayor and several others died from typhus contracted from a prisoner.

The risk of infection from gaols was known to the army and navy. In 1757 a naval surgeon, James Lind, later a Fellow of the Medical Society of London, who introduced lemon juice, for the prevention of scurvy, to the navy, realised that prisoners impressed into the navy brought gaol fever from London. The medical profession then knew nothing of the dangers of lice in spreading the disease, but they did know that clothing was infective and in 1774, when a Bill before Parliament outlined prison reforms, it omitted to mention that prisoners' clothing should be burnt. This omission was criticised by Lettsom in the *Gentleman's Magazine* of the same year.

The great pioneer of prison reform, Dr. John Howard, was a friend of Fothergill and Lettsom. He was much averse to personal publicity and stopped the movement by Lettsom and his friends for the erection of a memorial. However, after his death a statue by John Bacon was erected in St. Paul's Cathedral where it is today.

The death of Lord George Gordon from typhus in 1793 in Newgate Prison provided the occasion for a study of the epidemiology of typhus in a closed community. Lord George Gordon, leader of an anti-Catholic riot, had been convicted of libelling the government, survived his prison sentence, but was then unable to raise the bail and returned to gaol. Lettsom was asked to prepare a report with the keeper, Mr. Kirby, and the surgeon, Mr. Gillespy.

Prisons at that time were divided into courts. The nobility were housed on the State side, and commoners were accommodated in a debtors' or felons' court, women and men being sometimes separated. A prisoner had died of typhus on the State side some time before Lord George Gordon and the fever had spread to the female common felons' ward. He commented that precautions to prevent spread of the fever were adequate on the State side, with burning of pitch, sprinkling of vinegar and airing of the room. In the women felons' yard there were six with fever and one who had died the previous night. The rooms were aired but the women were in a distressful state of clothing and filth. On the commoners' side in the debtors' and felons' yard 250 men were confined but none with fever. Lettsom found it odd that the disease was most prevalent on the affluent side of the prison. He noted that there was a passage serving the women felons' yard and the State side court which at times was very crowded. He noted that half the women were removed to Woolwich en route to Botany Bay just before Lord George Gordon's death. He learnt that these women were attacked by typhus while in Woolwich. Lettsom concluded:

(1) Introduction of infection—typhus originated from contagion of effluvia from the human body. The State side prisoners and women felons were sharing a common passageway.

(2) Prevention of Infection—clothing should be provided capable of being washed and changed twice a week. Personal cleanliness was advocated and frequent washing of the whole body—by showering. The diet should be adequate with fresh foods and temperance should be salutary. Fresh air and exercise should be provided, even tennis. The bedding should be adequate and he designed an iron cot standing on legs for easy cleaning. The full report appears in "The Memoirs of the Medical Society of London, 1795, Vol. 4".

The jeweller, Mr. James Neild, was another great, if less famous, prison reformer by whose effort the pioneer work of Howard was kept alive. Neild was stimulated by the sermons of the Rev. William Dodd (later hanged for forgery) to found the Society for the Discharge and Relief of Persons imprisoned for Small Debts. Lettsom had been a friend of Neild for many years and persuaded him to publish his observations on prisons in the *Gentleman's Magazine* edited by Nichols, another friend. These articles were prefaced by Lettsom and published between 1803 and 1813, and had an enormous influence on the public and then on the gaols. The governors were thereafter on the alert for visits and their prisons were kept in readiness as never before.

Vaccination/Inoculation

In the eighteenth century one of the most prevalent medical problems was smallpox. In the Far East inoculation had been practised from the seventeenth century and is described by Lady Mary Wortley Montagu in a letter to her friend, Mrs. Sarah Chiswell, at home in England in 1717. She doubted whether physicians in England could be persuaded to adopt this method, as it would destroy a considerable source of their revenue. She supported her surgeon Maitland in his efforts to popularise the method and had her children inoculated. Inevitably an outbreak of smallpox occurred as a result of contact with an inoculated person. However, Robert Sutton and his son David took up the method and set up an inoculation centre at Ingatestone in Essex. Their method was successful and Baron Thomas Dimsdale probably learnt the technique from the Suttons. Dimsdale was a Quaker and when the Empress Catherine II of Russia decided to introduce inoculation to her Court, Fothergill recommended Dimsdale for the job. He inoculated the Imperial family satisfactorily for which he received rich rewards. His technique, using the serum from a vesicle early in its formation, was safer than the pustule commonly used, but necessitated the isolation of the subject and was done in special centres. Thus it was available only to the wealthy. Dr. Watkinson, a physician to the General Dispensary and a friend of Lettsom, set up a society for the inoculation of the poor in their own homes.

Baron Dimsdale opposed this general inoculation due to the risk of spreading the infection. Lettsom supported his friend Watkinson and published a pamphlet supporting general inoculation, but in this case Lettsom's arguments were wrong and Dimsdale and Lettsom became estranged. No doubt inoculation protected the individual who was successfully inoculated but the risks of spread of infection were great.

In 1783 Dr. John Haygarth of Chester and Bath proposed isolation hospitals for fever cases and the general inoculation of all the inhabitants of a town at intervals of two or three years. Unfortunately, these proposals were not taken up in spite of support by Lettsom and other influential people, but events overtook Haygarth's proposals in the form of vaccination. Jenner's work was based on the fact, known for many years, that people infected with cowpox were generally found to be protected from smallpox. Jenner's brilliance was in seeing that if cowpox caught accidentally prevented smallpox at a subsequent inoculation, cowpox deliberately given might also give protection. As Jenner was a pupil of Hunter he took his master's advice: why think, why not try the experiment? In 1796 a dairy maid, Sarah Nelmes, got cowpox and from one of the sores Jenner inoculated a boy, James Phipps. Six weeks later he inoculated the boy with smallpox which failed to affect

FIG. 10. Edward Jenner (1749–1857) Royal College of Physicians.

him. Jenner's paper was submitted to the Royal Society who advised against the procedure. He was not daunted, collected a few more cases, and published his famous enquiry in 1798.

He came to London to see the pamphlet through publication and while there was helped by Dr. William Woodville of the smallpox hospital. The medical profession was generally hostile, and prominent members of the Medical Society of London were regrettably unenthusiastic. Dr. Simms commented in harsh and unjustifiable language and Lettsom was sceptical. Help came from Dr. George Pearson at St. George's Hospital, a well known scientific figure, whose favourable pamphlet was accepted. Dr. William Woodville was a Quaker, a friend of Lettsom, and on the Council of the Medical Society of London. He adopted the method and both he and subsequently Lettsom became enthusiastic supporters. Dr. Woodville was even given a special passport at this difficult time to visit Paris and successfully demonstrated Jenner's method. Dr. Pearson became the leading proponent of vaccination in London and his name rapidly began to overshadow Jenner's, a cause of antipathy between the two men. Finally, in 1802, Parliament voted Jenner a grant of £10,000—very little in view of what Jenner had spent in launching his idea.

Lettsom sent a copy of Jenner's first pamphlet to his friend Benjamin Waterhouse, Professor of Medicine at the University of Cambridge (Harvard). (See p. 40). He was most impressed and wrote to Lettsom and other friends asking for supplies of lymph. He then vaccinated his own children, one of whom was then inoculated with smallpox which failed to develop. Waterhouse corresponded freely with Jenner, and Lettsom, who continued to supply lymph until the supplies were sufficient locally. Waterhouse finally managed to convince important people, including Jefferson, by demonstrating the safety of vaccination to the Boston Board of Health, and it was henceforth accepted throughout America.

Jenner was made a corresponding member of the Medical Society of London and awarded the last Fothergill gold medal of the Society in 1803 for the discovery of vaccination when he was "a member of no other literary society". The Royal Jennerian Institution was founded, assisted by the efforts of Lettsom, but due to internal dissension Jenner himself finally resigned from the board.

The anti-vaccinationists were active and included Dr. John Birch of St. Thomas's Hospital, Dr. Benjamin Moseley of the Royal Hospital, Chelsea, and Dr. William Rowley of the Marylebone Infirmary. Some of their arguments were extremely bizarre; Birch considered that smallpox was a merciful provision of Providence to lessen the burden of a poor man's family where the abundance of children exceeded the means of providing food and raiment for them; Moseley thought vaccination might confer some bovine characteristics on the recipient, a view held also by Rowley. These opinions were contested by Lettsom in his letters to the *Gentleman's Magazine* of 1808.

Jenner died in 1823 with glory and honours and within 30 years vaccination became compulsory in every country in Europe except his own, the last to enforce it in 1853.

Hospitals

Until mid eighteenth century, London had only two large hospitals, St. Bartholomew's and St. Thomas's but during the latter half all the great teaching hospitals were founded— Westminster, Guy's, St. George's, London, Middlesex, the Locke, and Queen Charlotte's. These provided some service for the treatment of the poor as in-patients. Care of the out-patient developed with the foundation of the dispensaries. The first of these was founded in 1769 in Soho Square for relief of the infant poor.

Lettsom was distressed that there was no provision for the sick poor in their own homes. He would often walk from his own house to that of Fothergill in Bloomsbury, through some of the poorest streets of the city. It was there that he decided to establish the Aldersgate Dispensary or General Dispensary for the relief of the poor in 1770. Patients were seen on the recommendation of one of the governors and could be visited at home.

The first physician appointed was Dr. Nathaniel Hulme (see Ch. IV), one of the founders of the Medical Society of London, and the success of the dispensary was largely due to his efforts. A surgeon, George Vaux, also a friend of Lettsom, was appointed and later a second physician, Lettsom himself. He devised a scheme for teaching on the dispensary out-patients much the same as that in use today, but it was not implemented until after the Apothecaries Act of 1815, which obliged any doctor prescribing or dispensing drugs to hold the licence of the Apothecaries. This gave the dispensaries their chance to start teaching, which they did with vigour, among them the General Dispensary, with Dr. Henry Clutterbuck (see Ch. IV) as physician and president of the Medical Society of London. This important contribution to medical education died out towards the mid-nineteenth century, the dispensaries declined, the General Dispensary moved and was eventually merged with St. Bartholomew's Hospital in 1932.

Dr. Richard Russel of Brighton was known as "Sea Water Russell" due to his work on the value of sea water in the care of enlarged glands, and his name is commemorated in many place names in Brighton. The fashion for sea-bathing grew after George III's recovery from insanity at Weymouth. Lettsom was impressed by this sea-water treatment and once again decided to try and apply it to his poor patients. With eight other prominent gentlemen, among them Mr. Adams who later became president of the Royal Humane Society, he established a charity in 1791 to found the Sea Bathing Infirmary at Margate. This hospital is perhaps Lettsom's main claim to fame, since it inspired the idea of open-air sanatoria, which spread widely throughout the world. He planned the solarium and verandah for sleeping on and arranged horse-drawn carts to take patients to the beach. The poor were transported to Margate from London by sailing boat or hoys and the education of children continued by the appointment of a schoolmaster at £25 p.a. This complete care of a patient was something quite new and owed much to Lettsom's detailed planning. The hospital was only open in the summer months and patients with non-pulmonary tuberculosis were treated, but the records also show patients with other conditions, especially osteomyelitis.

By 1858 the hospital was open the whole year and became the Royal Sea Bathing Infirmary, despite little support from

Fig. 11. A view of the Royal Sea-Bathing Hospital at Margate showing the statue of Erasmus Wilson in the foreground (*Miss Olive Monahan*).

the local people who were not admitted to the hospital for many years. Financial help came from the City Livery Com. panies and an association with the Foundling Hospital in Coram Fields. In the mid-nineteenth century electric light was installed and there was a heated pool and both fresh and sea water in the rooms. Erasmus Wilson (see Ch. IV), a president of the Medical Society of London, who introduced the Turkish Bath to England, donated £30,000 in 1833 towards a new block. and his widow placed a statue of him outside the hospital. In modern times Dr. Basil Armstrong continued the pioneering work, especially in treatment of orthopaedic tuberculosis, and had a commemorative plaque to Lettsom "The Friend of man" placed in the entrance hall.

The Society continued its interest in the development of hospitals and schools of medicine. In 1905 the Oration by Mr. Henry Morris (see Ch. IV) discussed at length the relations between the London hospitals and their affiliated medical schools which were in financial difficulties at the time. This led to protests by the anti-vivisectionists who said that endowed hospitals should not subsidise medical schools; it was urged that clinical and pre-clinical subjects should be taught by doctors.

After the 1914–18 war there was much dissension over the future of medical education and the role of the hospitals. In his powerful presidential address of 1919 Dr. Arthur Voelcker urged doctors to lead social reforms; he castigated the profession for inertia in developing their services and for their opposition to State medical services; professional standards should remain the criteria of progress and all aspects of medical and nursing care were the province of the doctor. Sir John Tweedy in his Oration the same year doubted if the advent of a Ministry of Health would effect all the good expected of it and some of the schemes would do no good at all—a cry reiterated to this day.

In 1924 it could be said by J. H. Waring (later Sir Hoburt Waring, see Ch. IV) in his Oration that the voluntary hospitals would remain and the profession would continue to practise as a profession and not a trade. The latter is still our ideal but is in danger of disappearing as did the voluntary hospital.

Royal Humane Society

It is remarkable that the methods for resuscitation in the late eighteenth century bear a close resemblance to those in use today. This is largely due to the influence of the Royal Humane Society, founded in 1774. The art of resuscitating the apparently dead does not seem to have been known to the ancients. The first recorded incident of apparent recovery from drowning in this country dates back to 1650. The great doctor Fothergill, friend of Lettsom, studied the problem and concluded that the methods of determining death were entirely wrong. In 1745

Mr. William Tossack resuscitated a man apparently dead from smoke suffocation by distending his lungs with air. Fothergill communicated a paper on this case to the Royal Society and concluded that it was possible to save life, but the medical world was unwilling to accept his theory as it was believed that life ended when breathing ceased.

In Europe Fothergill's paper attracted attention and in 1767 successful attempts at resuscitation were made in Switzerland. In the same year a society for the recovery of the apparently drowned was formed in Amsterdam. In London a surgeon, Dr. Thomas Cogan, translated the Amsterdam Society Transactions in 1773. The translation was studied by the apothecary, Dr. William Hawes, who offered from his own pocket a reward to those who brought the body of an apparently drowned person within a certain time of the accident to a reception centre, where resuscitation was tried. Dr. Cogan convinced Hawes that they should found a Humane Society, and thirty-two gentlemen joined the enterprise. Amongst them were Lettsom and Bancroft (see Ch. II), both Fellows of the Medical Society of London. Also named were Dr. Heberden, Dr. Bedde, Dr. Cooper, Dr. Ford and Dr. Kooystra and the great Dr. Oliver Goldsmith. The Lord Mayor of London, Mr. Frederick Bull, agreed to be the first president. The first minutes of 18th April, 1774 only mention sixteen names and Lettsom is not among them, but he was present on the 11th May and elected to the committee. Dr. William Hawes was strenuous in his efforts to achieve the success of the society, and the first volume of annual reports, dedicated to King George III, appeared in 1812. In this are numerous references to Lettsom, including his advice on the early judicious application of resuscitative means and a donation by him of 10 gns. annually for pious books for the restored.

There are articles and letters by Dr. Fothergill, though it is not always clear whether this is the famous John Fothergill or his relative, Anthony Fothergill, who practised first in Northampton then, after a spell in London, settled in Bath. Anthony Fothergill was undoubtedly the author of one communication, *Hints on Animation* in which he notes the scarcity of suitable apparatus and want of proper receiving houses. He notes cases of survival after 20 mins. submersion and yet death after 5 mins. under water. Later there is a long article on the value of dephlogisticated air, i.e. highly purified air, in resuscitation, no doubt inspired by Priestley's recent discovery of oxygen. He also discusses the use of electricity, quoting a man struck by lightning entirely restored by electrification skilfully performed by a practitioner of Guy's Hospital, and goes on to advocate the prudent application of heat. Certainly Anthony Fothergill deserves more credit and in his will he left £500 to the Royal Humane Society to endow a medal for efforts at resuscitation. This was first awarded to authors of works on saving life from drowning, but later given to schools and institutions for proficiency in life-saving.

The Royal Family were greatly interested in this work and in 1834 land was given to build a receiving house in Hyde Park to cope with the many cases of drowning in the Serpentine. A building stood on the same site until badly damaged in the Second World War. In 1806 the Emperor Alexander I of Russia received the gold medal of the Royal Humane Society for personally resuscitating one of his subjects drowned in the river Wilna although the English Dr. Weilly, who was present, advised that further effort was unlikely to succeed.

At first the Royal Humane Society concentrated on those apparently drowned and along the Thames sections were allocated to medical assistants responsible for resuscitation. Later the Society tackled any cases of accidental death, including poisoning and lightning.

Lettsom was active in the organisation of the Royal Humane Society and prepared the annual reports from 1808–1813, when Dr. T. Pettigrew (see Ch. IV), a Fellow of the Medical Society of London succeeded him. In the Royal Humane Society's office today is an engraving by Robert Pollard (1787) of a painting by Robert Smirk "Young Man Restored to Life". It shows Dr. Lettsom introducing the mother to the room where Dr. Hawes is sitting by the bed supporting the young man.

FIG. 12. Pollard's engraving (1787) of the painting "Young Man Restored to Life" by Robert Smirk, showing Lettsom with outstretched arm.

Most of the apparatus in use in 1774 is familiar today, with a bellows and curved tube for the nose or mouth. Less familiar would be the anal speculum which connects to a brass combustion chamber for burning tobacco, with a grill to prevent hot ashes passing into the rectum when the bellows is connected. This insufflation of the supposed stimulant tobacco smoke was condemned by John Hunter and later deprecated by Lettsom in 1812. The Medical Society of London concerned itself with the apparatus for resuscitation and held an exhibition in 1775. Although, as Lettsom wrote, "at the beginning the Royal Humane Society excited more ridicule than patronage", ever since then London medical men have given it support.

Cremation

We, the undersigned, disapprove the present custom of burying the dead and we desire to substitute some mode

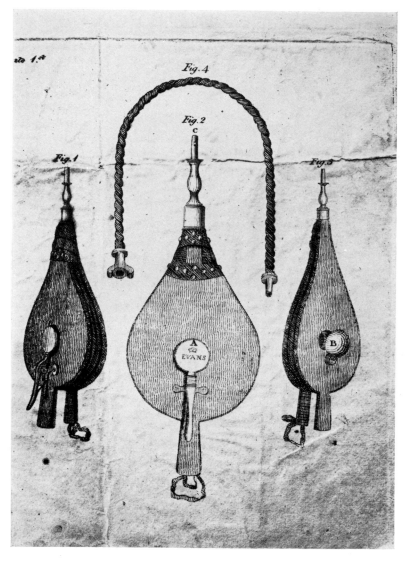

Fig. 13a

FIGS. 13a and 13b. Drawings of Resuscitation Apparatus used by the Royal Humane
Society in Lettsom's time (*Royal College of Surgeons*).

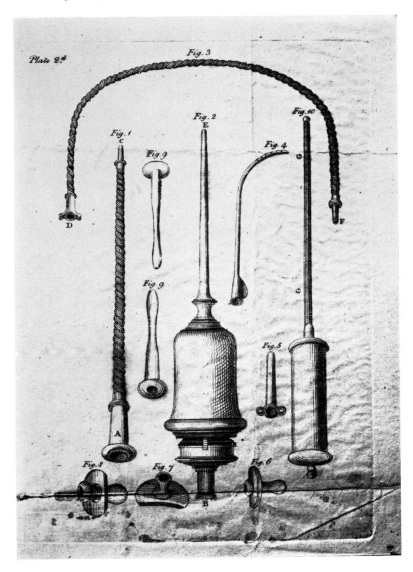

Fig. 13b

56

which shall rapidly resolve the body into its component elements, by a process which cannot offend the living and shall render the remains perfectly innocuous. Until some better method is devised we desire to adopt that usually known as Cremation.

This was the declaration drawn up and signed on 13th January 1874 by Sir Henry Thompson and fifteen of his friends.

Sir Henry Thompson, grandson of the painter Medley, a Fellow of our Society and Lettsomian lecturer in 1863. He was surgeon to Queen Victoria and crushed the bladder stones of Leopold I of Belgium and Napoleon III. He was a novelist, astronomer and gastronome celebrated for his "octaves"— dinner for eight, with eight courses, at eight o'clock.

Cremation was accepted in biblical times and generally adopted by the Greek and Roman civilisations. With the advent of Christianity and the belief in bodily resurrection, cremation fell into disfavour, but by the seventeenth century books appeared advocating this alternative to burial and discussion continued during the next two centuries.

Professor Brunetti of Padua exhibited a model of his cremating apparatus at the Vienna Exposition in 1873, where it was seen by Sir Henry Thompson. He returned to England to become the leading proponent of cremation. In 1874 he published a paper on the Treatment of the Body after Death, supporting cremation as a sanitary measure which would prevent premature burial, reduce the expense of funerals, spare the mourners exposure to the weather and preserve the ashes from vandalism—also, they might be used as fertiliser. The declaration was also signed by Sir T. Spencer Wells, John Everett Millais, John Tenniel and Anthony Trollope.

By this simple act the Cremation Society of England came into being, and was advised that cremation could be legally performed. Opposition from the Church delayed the establishment of a crematorium, which was finally built at Woking with a direct railway communication from Waterloo. In 1879 a horse was cremated there but opposition from the local population and the Home Office prohibited the use of the building.

In 1882 a Captain Hanham cremated his wife and mother in a crematorium on his own estate and in the following year the eccentric Dr. William Price, aged 83, attempted to cremate his infant son. He claimed to be a Druid High Priest and performed the rites dressed in a white tunic over green trousers. He was arrested, tried at Cardiff, and acquitted in 1884. This was the break-through that the Cremation Society awaited and the first official cremation took place at Woking in 1885. Sir Henry Thompson published his book "Modern Cremation" and in it were the forms required by the Cremation Society— substantially the basis of the forms used today.

In 1902 an Act of Parliament laid down regulations for burning human remains and enabled burial authorities to establish crematoria. In the same year the Golders Green Crematorium was opened by Sir Henry Thompson, president of the Cremation Society. He died in 1904 and his memorial is in the chapel at Golders Green.

The movement spread and was gradually accepted by State and Church. The bodies of distinguished persons destined for burial in Westminster Abbey must first be cremated and the first of these was Sir Henry Irving. In 1917 H.R.H. the Duchess of Connaught was cremated.

Lord Horder, president of the Medical Society of London in 1934, became Chairman of the Council of the Cremation Society in 1936, and President in 1940. During his term of office the Cremation Society gained the acceptance of the religious communities; in 1944 Archbishop Temple was cremated, and Archbishop Lang in 1946; by 1959 a Jewish Scroll of Remembrance was unveiled at Golders Green, recognising the growing practice of cremation among members of the Reform and Liberal Synagogues. Eventually in 1963 the Pope sanctioned cremation for Catholics.

The work of the pioneer, Sir Henry Thompson, followed by the able advocacy of Lord Horder, both prominent members

of the Medical Society of London, did much to achieve acceptance of cremation in this country today.

Ambulance

   The Ambulance Service as we know it is a very recent
development. Even in the nineteenth century transport of the
sick and injured to hospital was rudimentary and a matter for
private arrangement. For the poor there was little alternative
to a stretcher improvised from a shutter or hurdle wheeled on
a barrow over cobbled streets—a safer means of transport than
the cab used by the well-to-do, which was more likely to
aggravate the injury. The Franco-Prussian War of 1870 provided the stimulus to civilian organisations to improve their
service. The Forces, especially in Europe, had been much better
organised in moving the sick and wounded, and our relief
organisations brought back designs for stretchers and ambulances. Then the two-wheeled litter, of German design by Neuss,
and the horse-drawn ambulance were introduced, largely due
to the efforts of John Furley of the St. John's Ambulance
Association. In 1882 he proposed to the association that they
should organise a service especially for the transport of sick
from the suburbs and railway stations to central London
hospitals. He offered to lend his own horse-drawn ambulance
and, with the wheeled litter they possessed, formed the Invalid
Transport Corps for the Metropolis in 1883.

   The Medical Society of London was again active in promoting a new service. In January 1882 Benjamin Howard gave
details at a meeting of the Society of the service provided by the
London Hospital, showing designs for ambulances. He suggested that each London hospital should develop a similar
organisation for its district which would eventually become a
Metropolitan service available on request to the police. The
unequal distribution of hospitals in central London, where
3,500 beds out of 4,500 were within $1\frac{1}{2}$ miles of Charing Cross,
underlined the need to transport the sick over long distances.
At the same meeting the lamentable lack of transport after
railway accidents was stressed; a recent accident on the Great

Northern Railway was quoted where casualties had to be transported by cab to the Royal Free Hospital, there being no other form of conveyance. There was doubt about the best form of transport for the injured and Benjamin Howard thought the two-wheeled litter inadequate. From these efforts there arose a public meeting under the chairmanship of the Duke of Cambridge and wide interest was aroused.

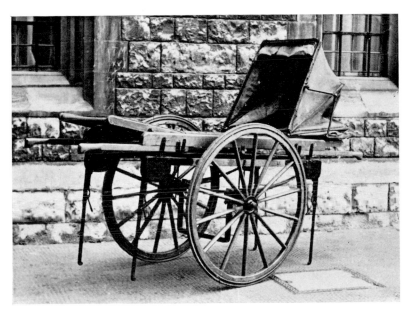

FIG. 14. A two-wheeled litter.

Since that time the transport of the sick and injured has been steadily improved with the development of local authority services. From time to time the Medical Society of London has discussed the subject and many Fellows have played a prominent role in the St. John's Ambulance Association.

Formation of the Royal Society of Medicine

A great dispute split the Medical Society of London at the end of the eighteenth century, leading to the foundation in

1805 of the Medical and Chirurgical Society of London which, a century later (1907), became the Royal Society of Medicine. The split was due mainly to irritation over the dominance of Dr. James Sims (see Ch. IV), who remained president continuously from 1786. He was the instigator of the expulsion of Whitehead in 1784, and soon after this membership of the Society sank so low that the question of dissolution was discussed. To the great credit of Sims he strenuously opposed such an idea, so strenuously in fact that he was challenged to a duel. He had been elected in 1786 out of his turn, and the rules were revised in 1787 so that he could continue to be president. Sims impressed Lettsom so much that in 1787 he gave to the society the freehold of No. 3 Bolt Court, Fleet Street, with the proviso that it should remain the property of the Society unless membership fell below twenty for six months (see also Ch. VII). It has never done so, but on the move from Bolt Court in 1850, when the Society amalgamated with the Westminster Medical Society, the trustees had to obtain the agreement of the descendants of Lettsom to have the proviso rescinded.

Sims engineered his re-election for 22 years. He decided who he would have on his council and also had them re-elected. Under him the Society flourished, partly due to relief from the financial burden of rent. They now had their own freehold property and indeed sub-let it. But younger men joining around 1800 began to get restive. The first discontent arose when Sims sold his library to the Society, asking £500 down and an annuity on the joint lives of himself and his wife of £60 and £90 a year to the survivor. The Society found that the volumes were only 6,000 in number (not 8,000 as promised) and several of the most valuable books were imperfect, in view of which Sims accepted an annuity of £15 a year.

Among the Fellows joining around 1800 were Astley Cooper, Henry Clutterbuck and John Yelloly—a major figure in what was to come. He was proposed by Philip Elliot, Lettsom's son-in-law, seconded by Lettsom and Sims himself. In 1805, at a meeting of the Council on February 18th, it was proposed that: "No gentleman shall be eligible for the office of President who shall have served in that capacity during the whole of the three preceding years." This was a direct challenge to Sims and the Council carried a resolution that: "A special General Meeting be called for this day five weeks for the purpose of considering the propriety of enacting the law respecting the President." Sims got busy and rescinded this last resolution on March 4th. This in turn was rescinded by the opposition on March 10th. The Council met on March 25th with Dr. Walsham in the chair. Sims was present but not Lettsom. Then William Saunders (later to become President of the Medical and Chirurgical Society) threw in his bombshell: Russell Square, March 18th, 1805,

> "Sir, as I have never attended the meetings of the (Council of the) Medical Society, and as I understand that a party has excluded from its Council some of the most learned and intelligent of its members, I beg to resign my seat as one of the Council, and thereby to decline the honour conferred on me by the Society." Wm. Saunders.

Six voted to accept the resignation and six against. The chairman gave a casting vote in favour of reconciliation and they all trooped off to the General Meeting. At this a resolution was carried that the president should hold the post for no more than three years but they referred it to a special meeting on April 29th for further discussion. On April 29th there were 79 members present, including Lettsom. At that meeting the resolution was put that the president should not hold office for more than three years. The ayes were 24, the noes were 47, 7 did not vote. Sims and his faction triumphed but the great split which nearly wrecked the Society had begun, and Yelloly resigned as trustee on 4th May.

William Saunders, Yelloly, Astley Cooper and Marcet were the real founders of the Medical and Chirurgical Society. They met in 1805; 26 secessionists from the Medical Society assembled at the Freemason's Tavern and formed themselves into a new society. One of their first rules was that "No gentleman be eligible to the office of President or Vice-President for more than two years in succession". Another was that "a certain number of the Council go out annually". The new society took a good many distinguished persons from the Medical Society of London, including Dr. Babington, Sir Wm. Blizard, Dr. Garthshore, Mr. Heaviside and Dr. Blane. Mr. Abernethy was an original member of the new society but he remained a member of the old. Throughout the year more members of the Medical Society resigned. Eventually Lettsom wrote on March 17th, 1806:

> Having early and uniformly given my support to the Medical Society, it may be presumed that I feel a cordial interest in its prosperity, and that I am not actuated by any sinister motive in the conduct I am resolved to adopt. On the last election of the Council a party having been convened professedly to unite in the expulsion of its most distinguished and literary members, and in the introduction of their own partisans, at a time when the society enjoyed general unanimity; I cannot consistently act with a Council constituted in this illiberal and party spirit, so subversive of the honour and harmony of the Society; and I do hereby resign my seat as member of the said Council.

The Council postponed acceptance and somehow or other persuaded Lettsom to withdraw. Sims must have felt that this was practically the end of his dictatorship but with the tenacity of the Irish he held on for another two years.

Finally, in 1808, Lettsom wrote to the Council suggesting an annual election of the president by ballot. This was the final touch and Sims resigned, sending a letter to the Society on November 11th, 1808:

> It having been asserted that discontents prevailed in the Society relative to the elections; and fearing that my being President was among the reasons for them, I beg leave to resign that office. He then gives an account of his stewardship of the Society, which indeed was remarkable, rescuing it from practically certain dissolution. In it he says, " Suffer

me now to take my leave, and to thank you for your constant attention and kindness to me".

He retired to Bath where he died in 1820.

A golden opportunity now presented itself for reconciliation with the Medical and Chirurgical Society, especially as the first militant president, Dr. William Saunders, had resigned. Matthew Baillie, a nephew of John Hunter, was then president of the Medical and Chirurgical Society, at which attendance had dwindled to less than ten. Dr. Good wrote on behalf of the Medical Society of London on December 16th, 1808 to Dr. Yelloly and as a consequence select committees of the two societies met on December 24th, 1808 to work out a basis for negotiation. Both societies wished to retain their names and places of meeting. The Medical Society of London urged its age and priority and certain legal difficulties over the Bolt Court property. The new Society was afraid it would seem to have been absorbed by its rival, the old aristocratic Medical Society would not yield. The conference broke down and the Societies decided to continue their friendly rivalry as before.

The Medical and Chirurgical Society continued to meet, first in Verulam Buildings, then at Lincoln's Inn, then at 53, Berners Street, for over fifty years. In 1899 it moved to Hanover Square and in 1905, after a conference at the Royal College of physicians, the Pathological Obstetrical, and Epidemological Societies united with it to form the Royal Society of Medicine.

Again the Medical Society of London decided to remain separate, Lettsom's gift of Bolt Court possibly being a stumbling block to union but not to friendly reconciliation.

One fact has consistently emerged from all the activities of the Society's first two hundred years, and it is the spirit which began with Lettsom, and was printed in the preface of Volume I of the "Memoirs" (1787): "Nothing has contributed more to the advancement of science than the establishment of the literary societies; these excite a generous ardour in liberal minds and raise even envy itself into useful emulation."

Chapter IV

Some Presidents and Orators of the Society

C. E. NEWMAN

Of the ten original founders of our Society, only four held office as president or orator. Of Lettsom, the most important, enough has been written elsewhere, but it is worth noting that he held back from the presidency until 1775, a troubled period, came in again in 1809 to restore confidence when James Sims was at last induced to retire, and was again president in 1813.

The second founder, president in 1776 and orator in 1777, was Nathaniel *Hulme* (1732–1807). A Yorkshireman who started, after apprenticeship to his brother, as surgeon's mate in the navy, he graduated at Edinburgh and wrote a thesis, published in 1768, showing that lime juice had been familiar to the English as treatment for scurvy since the sixteenth century. He was an obstetrician and first physician appointed to the General Dispensary set up in Aldersgate by Lettsom in 1770, and later a Licentiate of the Royal College of Physicians. Hulme took the chair at the first meeting of the Society on May 19th, 1773, which was probably held at his house in Mudford Court, Fenchurch Street, at which ten members were present. At the second meeting he was elected librarian, an office which Lettsom considered highly important in the Society. His Oration in 1777 was on a bladder stone he had broken up with salt of tartar and vitriol, a treatment he subsequently advocated in a book for scurvy, gout and worms as well. He was a Fellow of the Royal Society and wrote on luminous bodies and a brick from the site of Babylon; he is said to have died after climbing to inspect a damaged chimney and falling downstairs, or possibly off the roof. The third founder, Mr. Edward *Ford* (1746–1809) was never president, but secretary for many years and orator in 1799; he is briefly described in Chapter II.

George *Edwards* (1752–1823) was president for one year after Hulme's four. He was a political theorist who wrote "the Almighty has destined that I should discover the true system of human economy" and it is "conjectured that his sanity was imperfect". Forty-two of his books are in the British Museum, however, including two in French advising the revolutionaries how to manage their affairs.

The president from 1780–1782 was Samuel Foart *Simmons* (1750–1813), a psychiatrist who treated George III towards the end with rare sense and humanity. He published the first Medical Register (1779, 1780 and 1783) and was a member of nearly all the learned and philosophical societies.

It was perhaps inevitable that a society deliberately designed to bring together men of independent minds, mostly Dissenters, should disagree on the management of its affairs. In 1775, under the presidency of John *Millar* (1733–1805), there was a tremendous upheaval about which we know little, as the minutes were subsequently expunged. Millar, who was supposed to be giving the Oration, resigned and walked out with three others, leaving Dr. Sims and the rest in possession, taking the keys with him. Lettsom was made president and patched up the quarrel with Millar, who was an excellent physician (at the Westminster Dispensary) but an eccentric, irritable and asthmatic Scot. He wrote on asthma, among many other subjects and was an enthusiastic promoter of our Society.

In 1784 another controversial president was appointed—Dr. John *Whitehead* (1740–1804). Whitehead was a Moravian from Cheshire who became a Wesleyan and linen-draper in Bristol, then a Quaker. He started a boarding school in Wandsworth, was given £100 a year to travel abroad, and gained his M.D. at Leyden in 1780. On his return to London Lettsom arranged his appointment as physician to the London Dispensary and he joined the Medical Society, becoming president only two years later. But he was not a good mixer, failed to turn up at meetings, and tried to organise Quaker support for election to a vacancy at the London Hospital against another member Dr. John Cook. This led to his expulsion from the Society while he was president. Although he narrowly beat his rival for the job, he treated only one patient in three weeks and was tacitly replaced by Cook. A war of pamphlets followed, ending in Lettsom's resuming the presidency. Whitehead subsequently became Wesley's doctor and wrote an unofficial biography which provoked further legal proceedings, although he is buried in Wesley's vault and, as Johnston Abraham says, "there must have been something lovable in this hot-headed man" and his ejection from the Society ought never to have ocurred.

In 1786 Dr. James *Sims* (1741–1820) started his unique twenty-two years as president. Sims was the son of a dissenting minister in County Down. He qualified at Leyden, practised in Tyrone, and then moved to London as physician to the General Dispensary. He is described as "a good-humoured, pleasant man, full of anecdote, an ample reservoir of good things, and for figures and facts a perfect chronicle of other times. He had a retentive memory, but when that failed in any particular he referred to a book of knowledge in the shape of a pocket-book, from which he quoted with oracular authority". Under Sims the Society flourished. The following year the first volume of "Memoirs" (later to become "Transactions") appeared, covering the more important papers read at the meetings; it is a tribute to the Society's energy that Volume 6, the last to be published for some years towards the end of Sim's presidency, devotes over 300 pages to a questionnaire on the influenza epidemic of 1803. Orators during these years were a mixed collection: notably George *Wallis* (1740–1800), whose enthusiasm for the theatre led to his virtually being expelled from York after writing a satirical play and who was an early opponent of bleeding and purging, also editor of the second edition of "Motherby's Dictionary"; Gilbert *Thompson* (1728–1803), one of the original members of the Society and a Quaker

Fig. 15. James Sims (1741–1820). President 1786–90 (*Royal College of Physicians*).

Fig. 16. George Birkbeck (1776–1841). Orator 1810 (*Royal College of Physicians*).

Fig. 17. Henry Clutterbuck (1767–1856). President 1819–21, 1825, 1840 (*Royal College of Physicians*).

Fig. 18. John M. Good (1765–1827). Orator 1808 (*Royal College of Physicians*).

friend of Fothergill, who translated Homer and Horace; Mr. James *Ware* (1756–1815), who founded the Society for the Blind; Dr. George *Pinkard* (1768–1835), who established and ran the Bloomsbury Dispensary and became president of the Society in 1811; Joseph *Adams* (1756–1818), who began as an apothecary but, finding the business "destructive to his feelings" and admiring John Hunter, qualified in Aberdeen and later became L.R.C.P. Another apothecary turned physician to give the Oration under Sims was John Mason *Good* (1764–1827), who became a Fellow of the Royal Society, spoke thirteen languages, and translated the Book of Job and Lucreti us whilst walking from patient to patient. He was largely responsible for two influential books on medicine and an encyclopedia in 12 volumes, "The Pantologia".

In 1805 Sims resigned the presidency after a dispute over a proposal to limit the Chair to one year's tenure, but eventually, by a vote of 47 to 24 members, restored his hold for another three years. But only a month later 26 members met under Dr. William *Saunders* (1743–1817, see Ch. II) at the Freemason's Tavern and formed themselves into the Medical and Chirurgical Society (see Ch. III). Among these breakaway members was Dr. William *Babington* (1756–1833) of whom Munk says "History does not supply us with a physician more loved or more respected". Babington came from Londonderry and succeeded Dr. Saunders at Guy's Hospital until his City practice became so large that he resigned; his statue in St. Paul's was put up by public subscription. His colleague at Guy's Hospital, Dr. Henry *Clutterbuck* (1770–1856), was equally distinguished and remained with the Medical Society, took over when Sims finally gave up the chair in 1808 and behaved with great courtesy towards him. Clutterbuck started the Medical and Chirurgical Review, took a doctorate at Glasgow, and wrote and practised in St. Paul's churchyard, also lecturing at the General Dispensary. He died after being knocked down by a cab while returning from one of the Society's Orations, and was reputed to be the perfect participant in discussions during his 50 years' regular attendance.

Lettsom stepped into the breach after Sims resigned, and the Oration of 1809 was given by Dr. *Sayer Walker* (1748–1826), who is portrayed in the Medley picture (see Ch. II). He was followed by Dr. George *Birkbeck* (1776–1841), a Quaker from Settle who qualified in Glasgow, came to London and started the Birkbeck Institute. He succeeded Lettsom as physician to the General Dispensary, was simple, unassuming, and generally beloved, an enthusiast for "useful knowledge". In 1811 he was proposed as secretary, but a young member, Joseph *Pettigrew* (1791–1865) was put up in opposition. Pettigrew had joined the Society in 1808 while still an apprentice to John Taunton, a surgeon, Taunton thought this a good opportunity to make a stand against the dominance of the physicians; 29 out of 35 Orators had been physicians, and no surgeon had been president. Pettigrew was finally elected, despite the resignation of Clutterbuck as librarian and Good as the other secretary, foregoing the salary for the job of registrar (which he then assumed) in exchange for the right to live in the Society's house. Through Lettsom's influence he also became secretary of the Royal Humane Society and eventually vaccinated the princess Victoria. He was commissioned by the Duke of Sussex, whose surgeon he became, to catalogue the library at Kensington Palace, was a prolific author—notably of a useful Medical Portrait Gallery—and a considerable antiquarian.

Once again Lettsom saved the Society from breaking up over the scandal of Pettigrew's appointment by becoming president himself for the last time. Taunton, who had tried to win the election, was placated by the oratorship in 1815, and meetings doubled their attendance rate. Another surgeon who gave the Oration, in 1811, was William *Blair* (1766–1822 see also Ch. II), a Methodist and an expert on secret writing; he contributed a classic article on the subject to Rees' *Cyclopedia*, including an "inscrutable" cipher of his own, the key to which unfortunately appeared the same year (1819). The orator in 1818 was Dr. David *Uwins* (1780–1837) "a little man with a large head, of a highly nervous temperament, an amiable and gentle man" of vast erudition but "the worst speaker" that

FIG. 19. Thomas J. Pettigrew
(1791–1865). Orator 1819
(*Royal College of Physicians*).

FIG. 20. James Copland (1791–1870).
Orator 1822
(*Royal College of Physicians*).

FIG. 21. Henry Hancock (1809–
1880). President 1848–50
(*Royal College of Physicians*),

FIG. 22. Marshall Hall (1790–1857).
Orator 1845
(*Royal College of Physicians*).

J. F. Clarke ever had occasion to report. And yet he was one of the most prominent Fellows in the 1830s, became president in 1828, and was a distinguished writer. The following year (1820) a Quaker from Antrim, Dr. Thomas *Hancock* (1783–1849) gave the Oration. He wrote voluminously on plague, morals, peace and the doctrines of Immediate Revelation and Universal and Saving Light, and was an enthusiastic disciple of Locke. He was followed by Dr. James *Copland* (1791–1870), a Fellow of the College of Physicians and another indefatigable writer, producing single-handed a "Dictionary of Practical Medicine" "extraordinary . . . for its size, comprehensiveness, accuracy and learning". His successor Dr. Edward *Grainger* (1797–1824) was equally remarkable; having been turned down by Guy's Hospital, he set up his own school, the Webb Street School of Anatomy, which had become a success as a complete private school before he died of tuberculosis at the age of 27.

Thomas *Callaway* (1791–1848) was orator in 1821 and president in 1829. He had an enormous practice—bus conductors were said to have shouted "Anyone for Dr. Callaways?" —and delivered a memorable eulogium, in near darkness, to an audience including Sir Robert Peel on his former teacher and hero, Astley Cooper. The president in 1823 was Dr. William *Sherman* (1767–1861), physician to the Waterloo Road Children's Infirmary and to the Western Infirmary, later Charing Cross Hospital. John *Haslam* (1764–1844), who was orator in 1826 and president in the following year, had a remarkable career, first as an apothecary to Bethlem Hospital then, after a period at Cambridge, licensed to practise as a psychiatrist. He wrote on insanity—about the man "who stopped his ears with wool and, in addition to a flannel night-cap, usually slept with his head in a tin saucepan", and about the expert on bomb-bursting, lobster-cracking and lengthening the brain who deceived many learned doctors. Another eccentric orator (1828) and president (1831) was Dr. John *Burne* (1796–1866); he started the myth of the evils of constipation, which he demonstrated was the cause of pretty well every known disease. This condemned the English-speaking world for ninety years until Prof. Witts blasted the theory, in 1937 with an article entitled "Ritual Purgation in Modern Medicine".

Walter Cooper *Dendy* (1794–1871), known as "the literary surgeon", gave the Oration in 1835 and was president in 1846. He was surgeon at Guy's Hospital and the Waterloo Road Dispensary, but his fame rests on his writings—prose and poems about dreams and illusions, skin diseases, travel, topography and philosophy. He illustrated his own books and after his retirement spent his time in the British Museum Reading Room; in 1867 he attacked Darwin at the Anthropological Society.

Henry *Hancock* (1809–1880), who became President of the Royal College of Surgeons in 1872, gave the Oration in 1842 and was president in 1848. He was an early surgeon at Charing Cross Hospital, one of the founders, chief ornaments and Dean of its medical school, and a great oculist. He performed the first successful operation for peritonitis due to disease of the appendix. In 1844 the Oration was given by Thomas *Bell* (1792–1880) on the microscope in medicine, a very advanced subject for the time. He was also a distinguished zoologist, Fellow of the Royal Society, and largely responsible for its removal to Burlington House. He retired to Gilbert White's house in Selborne and produced a classic edition of the "Natural History".

In 1845 the Oration was given by Dr. Marshall *Hall* (1790–1857), who came from a family of inventors; his father was the first to use chlorine for bleaching cotton. Hall's first important work was a paper on blood-letting (1824) which started the revolution against this treatment. His work on the physiology of the capillaries was refused by the Royal Society in 1831, but enthusiastically approved in Germany, as was his discovery of reflex action—also refused as "frivolous" by the Royal Society. No hospital in London would appoint him, but he made an enormous success of private practice. He devised a system of artificial respiration, helped to abolish open railway carriages, the flogging of soldiers and slavery in America— altogether one of the most remarkable of British medical men.

The amalgamation of our Society with the Westminster Medical Society has been described in Chapter I. The surgeon whose commanding presence and pleasant personality were a great help in this manoeuvre was Francis *Hird* (1813–1888) of Charing Cross Hospital. Founder of Epsom College, he was orator in 1848 and 1850, gave the Lettsomian lecture in 1855, and became president of both societies. Two other influential figures in the amalgamation and the move from Bolt Court to Hanover Square were Sir James Risdon *Bennet* (1809–1891), who was president in 1850 and ultimately president of the Royal College of Physicians, and William Dingle *Chowne* (1791–1870), both Edinburgh graduates. Chowne became physician to the Charing Cross Hospital, was orator in 1841 and, after the presidency of the Westminster Medical Society, was elected to that of our Society in 1856. On Hird's retirement, Dr. Edward *Murphy* (1802–1877) from Dublin became president Murphy was the first to give chloroform for labour in London, and became Professor of obstetrics at University College Hospital.

The presidency of the new combined society changed from a two to one-year tenure, alternating between physicians and surgeons, and the meetings flourished, with attendances of 90 under the presidencies of Bennet and Murphy. Fellows of the Royal College of Physicians, once a rarity among members, steadily increased in number; the influence of Dissent faded as the general emancipation of religious sects became effective and the rigour of the Quakers lessened. The presidency tended to go to eminent names rather than faithful members of the Society and the Fothergillian Gold Medal, previously awarded in an open essay competition, was finally given as an honour for medical distinction. There were many distinguished orators and presidents during this period: Edwin *Canton* (1817–1885), surgeon at Charing Cross Hospital and first-class ophthalmologist, friend of Huxley and contributor to *Punch*, who was found dead on Hampstead Heath with a bottle of prussic acid in his hand; John *Snow* (1815–1858), well-known as a pioneer in public health and anaesthesia, giving chloroform to Queen

Victoria in labour and discovering the water-born infection of cholera; Edward *Headland* (1803–1869), a general practitioner, among the first to insist on payment for service rather than medicines and to abandon massive drugging; Henry *Smith* (1823–1894), fisherman, naturalist and scholar as well as surgeon at King's College Hospital, who introduced the clamp and cautery method of dealing with piles, displeasing the profession by saying that "haemorrhoids are a magnificent source of income"; an effective president (1867), Smith was kindly and humorous and effective at a difficult period for the Society.

Two Society figures of this period contributed to the respectability of reporting: Forbes Benignus *Winslow* (1810–1874), whose portrait hung in the Society's House, reported for *The Times* in the House of Commons while a student and wrote several books on insanity. He was the first to maintain that suicide was a mental illness rather than a crime, opened two private and humane asylums, and founded the *Quarterly Journal of Psychological Medicine;* and James Fernandez *Clarke* (1812–1875), a general practitioner, who was for thirty years chief reporter for the *Lancet.* He was a wonderful observer and in his old age wrote about the Society in his "Autobiographical Reminiscences". Sir Benjamin Ward *Richardson* (1828–1896) was president in 1868 and known for his invention of 14 anaesthetics; he also wrote on domestic sanitation and euthanasia for animals, was an early cycling enthusiast and a strong teetotaller. The following year the president was John *Hilton* (1805–1878), the famous author of "Rest and Pain" (1863); he also made the dissections, at Guy's Hospital, from which Towne's inimitable wax models were made, and became President of the Royal College of Surgeons in 1867.

John Louis William *Thudichum,* (1829–1901), qualified in Giessen and settled in London in 1853. He had a most successful practice, lectured in chemistry (he had studied under Liebig) at St. Thomas' Hospital, and constituted a sort of one-man Medical Research Institute under Sir John Simon at the Privy Council. He gave the oration in 1864, was a member of many societies, and suffered from being an authority on most

FIG. 23. William Dingle Chowne
(1791–1870). President 1856–57
(*Royal College of Physicians*).

FIG. 24. John Snow (1815–1858).
President 1855–56
(*Royal College of Physicians*).

FIG. 25. John Hilton (1805–1378).
President 1859–60
(*Royal College of Physicians*).

FIG. 26. Isaac Baker Brown
(1812–1872). President 1865–66
(*Royal College of Physicians*).

subjects. He was little regarded in his own time as a scientist, being in fact, far ahead of his time, but when Otto Rosenheim discovered 300 odd preparations of pure substances from the brain and other biological material in the stables of Thudichum's old home, it became obvious that he had been a chemical researcher of the first order. He has again suffered from rather silly books written by journalistic admirers, but in the end, he will be acknowledged.

In 1865 came the presidency of the unfortunate Isaac Baker *Brown* (1812–1873). He played a leading part in the foundation of St. Mary's Hospital and was appointed its first surgeon-gynaecologist. He did first-class work on ovarian cysts, but late in life was seized with the conviction that removal of the clitoris was the cure for hysteria, epilepsy and most of the disorders of women. The operation was unjustifiable, and caused him to be expelled from the Obstetrical Society. Until 1865 at least, he seems to have been *persona grata* at the Medical Society, but he died almost destitute. Sir Andrew *Clark* (1826–1893), was the first president to our society (1871) to become subsequently president of the Royal College of Physicians. After an early career in the navy, he became physician to the London Hospital and a friend of the Gladstones; he was precise and serious, turned to theology for recreation, and may have been the original of Sir Faraday Bond.

The president in our centenary year was the solemn figure of Dr. Samuel Osborne *Habershon* (1825–1889). He was appointed demonstrator of anatomy and tutor at Guy's Hospital before he had taken his M.D. and remained there most of his life, until a disagreement over nursing led to his resignation in 1880. He was very religious, one of the founders of the Christian Medical Association, and held many offices in the Royal College of Physicians. The centenary Oration, delivered by Dr. John *Cockle* (1813–1900), was on Recent Doctrines concerning the Mind, and in true Victorian spirit paid no particular attention to the Society's past. Two orator-presidents at this time served in the Crimea: Frederick James *Gant* (1825–1905), who did a great deal for the Royal Free

Hospital, showed that prize cattle were winning because of fatty degeneration, and wore Crimean-period clothes and whiskers to his death; he inscribed on his wife's tombstone "To the unspeakable distress of her husband, his age and bodily affliction debar him from ever visiting her grave, at a distance of 10 miles from London"; Robert Brudenell *Carter* (1828–1918), named after Cardigan's father, wrote on hysteria and diseases of the nervous system; he took part as an ophthalmologist in founding several eye hospitals, wrote for the *Lancet* and *The Times*, where he was the first person to use a typewriter, and famous for wearing two pairs of spectacles.

Sir Erasmus *Wilson* (1809–1884) was orator in 1876 and president in 1878. After an erratic education, he was advised by Thomas Wakley to devote himself to skins—so closely that when he entered a room the company would scratch themselves! He became unquestionably the top authority on this subject and made a colossal fortune, with which he paid for Cleopatra's Needle to be brought to London and endowed many charities. He is said to have been the instigator of the English habit of having regular baths, to have introduced Turkish baths and courageously helped Wakley to get flogging in the army abolished. He was never on the regular staff of a great hospital, but was one of the original Fellows of the Royal College of Surgeons, of which he became president in 1881.

An even more remarkable man was John Hughlings *Jackson* (1835-1911), certainly the greatest neurologist of his century and possibly the greatest scientific clinician. He was a Quaker, serious and withdrawn, with little interest in everyday affairs or gift for expression, but he inspired almost every neurologist in every country. It is said that he read thrillers, with the backs torn off, as he drove round in his carriage, so perhaps his Quakerism was less rigorous than appeared. He gave the Oration in 1877 and was president in 1888. The orator that year was Sir Joseph *Fayrer* (1824–1907), who started in the Merchant Navy, qualified at Charing Cross, Rome and Edinburgh, then had a brilliant career in India as Professor of

Surgery at Calcutta and surgeon to the Viceroy before retiring to lead an equally busy life in London. He was a great sportsman and linguist, and interested in poetry, science and theology. William Miller *Ord* (1834–1902) was physician at Guy's Hospital and associated with the discovery of myxoedema —a name he invented. He was a botanist, geologist and scholar, did good work on colloids, and was responsible for the revival of the medical school at Guy's Hospital. He was president in 1885 and orator in 1894.

In 1888 the president was Sir William *Mac Cormac* (1836–1901) from Belfast, who served as a surgeon in the Franco-Prussian war; he was the only man to see Napoleon III creep into Sedan, and after the battle among the first to apply Listerian principles to military surgery. After working at St. Thomas's Hospital in London he was off again in 1876 to the Turko-Servian war and acted as a brilliant secretary to the Seventh International Congress in 1881. After holding the presidency of the Royal College of Surgeons for four years, he served in the Boer War; his tall handsome appearance and energy did much to internationalise English surgery. He was followed as president of our Society by Charles Theodore *Williams* (1838–1912), the leading authority on tuberculosis at the end of the century and physician to St. George's Hospital and the Brompton hospitals, during the period when high-altitude and sanatorium treatment began. Williams is also remembered for his foundation of four scholarships at Pembroke College, Oxford—one in anatomy, one in physiology and two in pathology.

Sir George Murray *Humphrey* (1820–1896) is also worth noting; he gave the Oration in 1885, and was one of the revivers of the Cambridge medical school while surgeon at Addenbrook's Hospital and Professor of Surgery. He was the first to restore the suprapubic approach to the bladder, which had been taboo, and declined the presidency of the College of Surgeons. He always looked ill, and it was he whom an examination candidate seized by the beard as he sat resting and said "What is the matter with you, my man?"

FIG. 27. Robert Brudenell Carter (1828 1918). President 1886–87.

FIG. 28. Sir Joseph Fayrer (1824–1907). President 1883–84.

FIG. 29. Sir James Crichton-Browne (1846–1938). President 1895–96.

FIG. 30. Sir Alfred Pearce Gould (1852–1922). President 1902–3.

One of the most extraordinary doctors of all time was Sir Jonathan *Hutchinson* (1828–1913), described as both a specialist in most subjects and the greatest general practitioner in Europe. He lectured in hospitals, societies, in the Polyclinic (one of the first post-graduate schools in London), and at his home in Haslemere, which became a sort of miniature university, as well as at the Royal College of Surgeons, of which he was president in 1889. He was the last of the great Quaker doctors, although he really lived by a new religion of his own devising, which substituted belief in evolution for personal salvation, and was known as a leading authority on syphilis, ophthalmology, dermatology and neurology. His vast collection of pathological drawings went to the John Hopkins School. His Oration was in 1889; two years later Sir Joseph *Lister* himself gave the Oration, having founded what became the Lister Institute in that same year.

In 1892 it was given by Sir James Crichton *Browne* (1846–1938)—first of the great members of the Society within living memory. He had been Medical Superintendant at the Wakefield Asylum and started an organic approach to the nature of insanity. When he came to London in 1875 others followed, and, with Jackson and Ferrier, he founded *Brain*. He became president in 1895, succeeding Sir William *Dalby* (1840–1918), a pioneer in training the deaf and dumb and an aural surgeon with the largest practice in London. He was the first to remove exostoses from the external meatus, although he never did a radical mastoid, and was a patron of the arts and fashion. The orator under his presidency was Sir Alfred Pearce *Gould* (1852–1922), then at the height of his career. Son of a Baptist minister and himself a teetotaller (though charming host) and a dogmatic and brilliant teacher, he was a follower of Sir Mitchell Banks. As surgeon at the Middlesex Hospital he was concerned with work on cancer, served in the 1914–18 war and supported many good causes. His presidency in 1902 followed that of Sir William Henry *Allchin* (1846–1912) who had a long and distinguished career as physician and dean at the Westminster Hospital. He resigned his appointment as

Assistant Registrar to the Royal College of Physicians in disapproval of its application to confer degrees, and worked towards the reconstitution of the University of London. He became physician to George V.

The orator for 1897, following Allchin, was Edmund Blackett *Owen* (1847–1915). At first an opponent of Lister, he was surgeon at St. Mary's Hospital, a most attractive if outspoken teacher and a man whose genial honesty did much to compose differences at the Royal College of Surgeons and in the reorganisation of the B.M.A. in 1900. He also smoothed over difficulties between St. John's Ambulance and the Red Cross during the First World War. Two years after him the Oration was given by Alban H. G. *Doran* (1849–1927), who has one of the longest bibliographies in the Royal College of Surgeons, where he made the best collection of auditory ossicles. He began his career in the museum there, became surgeon to the Samaritan Hospital, and after failing eyesight forced his retirement, returned to catalogue the collection of instruments. The orator in 1900 was Sir James Kingston *Fowler* (1852–1934), physician at the Middlesex and Midhurst Hospitals, an authority on tuberculosis, who served on various governmental medical committees and eventually became Warden of Hayles and Beaulieu Abbeys.

John *Langton* (1839–1910), who was president in 1904, was born on the site which became King's College Hospital. A fine tall man, strict Sabbatarian but humane clinical teacher, he was surgeon at St. Bartholomew's Hospital and for 43 years attended the City of London Truss Society on six mornings a week, where he saw over a quarter of a million cases of hernia. His successor as president was Sir Thomas Lauder *Brunton* (1844–1916), a Scot who made the independent, if not the first, discovery of the action of amyl nitrate on angina. He became physician to St. Bartholomew's Hospital and a great authority not only on pharmacology but also on non-medicinal forms of treatment. He had a most successful practice and a conspicuous career in the Royal College of Physicians.

The orator in 1905 was a remarkable man, Sir Henry *Morris* (1844–1926), of Welsh-Jewish ancestry. He graduated in philosophy at University College, qualified at Guy's Hospital and became surgeon to the Middlesex Hospital. He was mainly an anatomist until, in 1880, a girl servant made history and two reputations by having a stone in the kidney diagnosed by Dr. Sydney Coupland and removed by Henry Morris. It was the first time diagnosis had been made clinically, and its author was nicknamed "Kidney Soupland". This made Morris's name and started him on his career as a urologist. He was also an authority on cancer, a considerable exponent of medical education and politics, and became president of the Royal College of Surgeons.

Professor Emil Theodor *Kocher* (1841–1917) followed Morris as orator in 1906. He was the first great thyroid surgeon, who claimed to have discovered *Cachexia Strumipriva*—myxoedema as a result of removal of the thyroid—although Gull had done so ten years earlier in 1873. Kocher was the only foreigner, except Harvey Cushing, to give the Oration. The presidency that year was held by Sir Charles *Ballance* (1856–1912), who performed the first modern radical mastoid operation as aural surgeon at St. Thomas's Hospital. He was the first experimental surgeon in the Hunterian tradition, chiefly on arteries and the repair of nerves, and became surgeon to the Metropolitan Police.

In 1908 the president was Charles Barrett *Lockwood* (1856–1914), a shy man who compensated with a sarcastic tongue. He was the first to lecture on bacteriology, at St. Bartholomew's in 1890, and wrote a book on aseptic surgery (1896). He was the first surgeon at St. Bartholomew's to wear gloves for operating, but died from septicaemia after pricking his finger at a peritonitis operation, because he had no carbolic in his glove. The following year the Oration was given by Sir Humphrey Davy *Rolleston* (1862–1944), who became president in 1926. The son of the Professor of physiology at Oxford, he was educated at Cambridge and St. Bartholomew's and became physician at St. George's and to George V. He succeeded Allbutt as Regius Professor at Cambridge and became president of the Royal College of Physicians for four years in 1922. He was a very good writer, medical historian, clinician and tennis-player, with an astonishing capacity for hard work and attention to detail; he always corresponded, in microscopic handwriting, on postcards.

William Henry *Battle* (1855–1936) was orator in 1910 and is immortalised as the originator of the incision for appendectomy; he was surgeon at St. Thomas's Hospital. The following year the president was John Mitchell *Bruce* (1846–1929), who studied at the Middlesex Hospital and in Vienna and became physician at the Charing Cross Hospital, where he was said to have been the most brilliant teacher in his day. He wrote a famous book on therapeutics. He was succeeded as president by Sir William Watson *Cheyne* (1852–1932), a formidable person. After a highly successful student career despite incipient tuberculosis, he was invited by Lister to be his house surgeon, subsequently acting as assistant and anaesthetist and doing much to promote Lister's principles. He was persistent in everything he did, presided over the Royal College of Surgeons during most of World War I, and after retirement went into parliament.

Sir John *Bland-Sutton* (1855–1936) was another to make his way by hard work and character; starting at the last of the private anatomy schools (Cooke's) and keeping himself by coaching, he went on to the Middlesex Hospital and was taken up by Morris. He deliberately took a job as surgeon there which obliged him to work through the summer holidays and gave him the opportunity to become a consummate operator. He made a huge fortune with which he was very generous to the hospital, building the Institute of Pathology, equipping the chapel and largely providing the playing-fields. He also built onto his house in Brook Street a hall in facsimile of Ahasuerus' palace at Susa, equipped with table silver which is still in use at the Royal College of Surgeons, of which he became president. He bore a resemblance to Napoleon, of which he was not unaware, and was a colourful president of the Society in 1914. In the same year the Oration was given by Sir Robert *Jones*

(1858–1933), the nephew, pupil and successor of that greatest of all orthopaedists Hugh Owen Thomas. He practised in Liverpool, where he did wonderful work on casualties during the digging of the Manchester Ship Canal and, with Dame Agnes Hunt, on the open-air treatment of bone disease. A genial, energetic man, he established orthopaedic surgery as a specialty and used it during the First World war. The year before war broke out had seen the presidency of Sir David *Ferrier* (1843–1928). He was a Scot who, after being a general practitioner, physiologist, professor of forensic medicine and physician, finally found himself as a neurologist and did the first work on cerebral localisation at King's and Queen Square Hospitals. He was a neat little man with bright and bird-like eye, the greatest neurologist in England of his day.

In 1916 Sir D'Arcy *Power* (1855–1941) became president. Son of a surgeon, he became surgeon at St. Bartholomew's Hospital and one of the best and most productive of medical historians, writing 23 volumes of archives, bibliography, portraiture and biography, and editing mediaeval texts. He was member of most and president of many societies, and largely concerned with the new Freemasons' Hospital and the Cooperative Wine Society. The same year the Oration was given by Sir *St.Clair Thomson* (1859–1943), who became president in 1917. He had an extraordinary career, starting as apprentice to his brother in Peterborough and then as ship's medical officer. He tried obstetrics and travelling with the rich, then laryngology, which he studied in Austria and Germany, and was finally appointed to King's College Hospital. He was then attacked by tuberculosis of the larynx, and remained mute for six months, filling in the time by noting every Shakespearean reference to medicine, on which he delivered his 64-page Oration—most occupy a mere eight or nine pages in the *Transactions*. On his recovery he became world-famous, with the King and most of the stage as his patients, a figure of great distinction and good looks who drove a yellow Rolls-Royce and danced until he was about eighty, dispensing princely hospitality.

Sir William *Osler* (1849–1919) demands far greater space than can be given here and is too well-known to need more than a mention that he gave the Oration in 1917, having declined in 1915 because of the war. He provides a fitting climax to nearly a decade of glorious distinction for the Society.

Theophilus Bulkeley *Hyslop* (1864–1936), gave an astonishing Oration in 1918. He was an Edinburgh graduate and superintendant of Bedlam, painted well, wrote considerable music, was a poet, "far above amateur level" at billiards; his books were said to embody "a greater variety of subject-matter than was good for any reader's digestion". His Oration blasted Schoenberg, the Post-Impressionists and German Kultur and he wrote, in the same year as "Mental Handicaps in Golf", a book entitled "Mental Handicaps in Art". The following orator was Sir John *Tweedy* (1849–1924), the first ophthalmologist to be president of the Royal College of Surgeons and the last surgeon to use a brougham. A kindly, modest man with a wheezing respiration, he was a bibliophile and musician, was offered the editorship of the *Lancet*, and orated on Tradition in Medicine.

The president in 1920 was Sir William *Hale White* (1857–1949), son of "Mark Rutherford" the Victorian novelist and translator of Spinoza. He was physician at Guy's Hospital and famous as the author of "Hale-White", the standard book on *materia medica*, pharmacy, pharmacology and therapeutics, a bible of the pre-chemotherapeutic age.

Lord *Dawson* (1864–1945) was orator in 1921 and president in 1922. In his day easily the leader of the profession: he would have been of whatever field he had chosen. He was splendid-looking, with a genius for knowing what the patient or the public wanted and what was possible—hence his usefulness as an adviser to George V and as president of the Royal College of Physicians, which he completely transformed. In 1918 he put forward in his Cavendish Lecture the first plan for a National Health Service; his Oration was on mucous colitis, the most popular subject of the day, and his presidential address, on Certain Developments in Medicine, showed extraordinary foresight as to what was to come. The orator to follow him was Sir Holburt *Waring* (1866–1941), a powerful, abrupt and frightening man and a great figure at St. Bartholomew's, the University of London, and the Royal College of Surgeons, of which he was president. He orated on the development of hospital care for all classes of the population. Ten years after, the Oration fell to Sir James *Berry* (1860–1946), who had failed to get the surgeoncy at St. Bartholomew's Hospital and started with the misfortunes of a short leg, and a cleft palate. But he became surgeon to the Royal Free Hospital, operated on cleft palates and thyroid, and held unusual but wise views on vast operations for incurable cancer and excessive operation for appendicitis and tonsils; he published mistakes as well as successes and was also a notable archaeologist; he held the presidency in 1931.

This brings the story down to 1923—the first hundred and fifty years of the Society's notable figures, or some of them; it would be difficult to see those of later date in proper perspective, and many are still alive. The photograph on page 87 shows some of the presidents who have held office since 1944 and were present in May 1971 at the Society's House when plans for the bicentenary were formulated. Many of our predecessors whom there is no space to mention were men of endearing eccentricities, men chosen for their office because of their personal as well as medical distinction. But an extraordinary number were distinguished also in other fields; no profession can boast such versatility as the medical.

Of the past presidents and orators at least a dozen were conspicuous as writers, notably J. M. Good, Henry Reeve, Pettigrew, J. F. Clarke, R. B. Carter and Sir John Tweedy. Nathaniel Hulme and Sir James Berry were good archaeologists and John Sims, Willshire and Ord were all good botanists. William Blair was one of the greatest cryptographers, and Wallis a competent dramatist. T. B. Hyslop and Willshire were good painters, and Mason, Roberts and Owen fine musicians. Several were classical scholars, notably Gilbert Thomson, and four were outstanding linguists: Good, Willshire,

Leared and Fayrer. Bradley was our only notable mathe-
matician, but there were four by no means negligible theo-
logians—Hancock, Dendy, Habershon and Sir Andrew Clark.
Sir William Bennett and Herbert Spencer were outstanding
connoisseurs, and F. Sibson and Clinton Dent outstanding
mountaineers.

Many held an astonishing range of interests—apart from
Hyslop, one may note B. W. Richardson, Thudichum, F. J.
Gant and W. M. Ord. And five were notable philanthropists—
James Ware, George Birkbeck, Marshall Hall, Erasmus
Wilson and Pearce Gould—on the model of our great and
generous founder Lettsom. Any society could be proud of these

Presidents 1950-1970

Back Row: Sir R. Bodley Scott, Sir Edward Muir, H. Thompson, Sir R. Drew,
Lord Brock, J. Smart. *Seated:* R. D. Wright, Sir Eric Riches, A. Douthwaite,
P. Maxwell Ellis, Cuthbert Dukes, Thomas Hunt, Sir Cecil Wakely, R. Cove-
Smith, W. Oakley.

men—and fond of them, with their oddities: James Sims with his fund of stories, Fernandez Clarke with his chatty reminiscences, Browne with "Picadilly weepers" that would put young men today to shame, Rolleston with his postcards, Thomson with his princely style of living, Bland-Sutton with his Assyrian palace . . .

The principal sources for these short biographies have been Munk's "Roll of the Royal College of Physicians" and Plarr's "Lives of the Fellows of the Royal College of Surgeons". Where these failed, the Medical Directories from 1845 give official details and enabled me to look up obituaries in the *Lancet* and *British Medical Journal*. E. Symes Thomson's Oration of 1882 gives many details, so does J. F. Clarke's "Autobiographical Reminiscences". Johnston Abraham's life of Lettsom is a mine of information about the early members of the Society. The "Dictionary of National Biography" often gives space to those, such as obstetricians, who are not in obvious medical sources. Mr. Bishop's Biographies in the library of the Royal College of Physicians contains some further information, so does the desultory reading of the Harveian librarian and the trained and inexhaustible mind of Mr. L. M. Payne, MBE to whom I am deeply indebted.

Chapter V

The Society's Library

G. B. Woodd-Walker

When John Coakley Lettsom and his medical friends founded the Medical Society of London the formation of a library was an integral part of his plan. There were few journals; doctors met and discussed cases but their sources were still the classical books of Galen and Hippocrates, and herbals. Lettsom had a fine library of his own at Grove Hill, Camberwell of 12,000 volumes. When, through his excessive generosity he fell on evil days and had to meet his creditors, he was obliged to sell his house and clear out his books. Many came to the Society in addition to those he had already given, and many of the Fellows also contributed to the new library.

In his pamphlet "Hints for the establishment of a Medical Society of London" Lettsom writes: "It is remarkable that among the different associations which have been established in the metropolis a Society for founding a medical library for the use of its respective members has been so little attended to. An institution of this kind is so apparently useful and interesting to those who are desirous of obtaining an easy access to the best ancient and modern authors that it requires no apology for the promotion of a medical library".

The catholic view of our founder aimed to include in his Society all those practitioners, physicians, surgeons and apothecaries whose aim and occupation was to advance the treatment of the sick. And this unity of purpose covering all the branches of medicine has been the character of our Society and its library ever since. Dr. Lettsom was not alone. Dr. Nathaniel Hulme (see Ch. IV), a co-founder, and the first honorary librarian, held office for 3 years. He also contributed books in the early years of the Society. It was Dr. Hulme who arranged the library and drew up the rules for its successful administration.

In 1776 the Medical Library of London was established and a committee of six was appointed by the Society. The rules were printed and circulated to every member of the College of Physicians and to the surgeons and apothecaries resident in London. We know the times of opening, the fines, and that a book was kept for suggestions for buying new works; evidently it was all efficiently arranged and well administered, and these rules, with only minor modifications in fines and times of opening, have continued to the present day. It is difficult to find informative references to the museum which was then in existence. The care of the museum was from earliest times entrusted to the librarian, and no member of the Society was allowed to remove any specimen. It seems likely that it was, as was John Hunter's, a collection of natural history and botanical specimens in keeping with the wide interests of Lettsom and his friends, but no remnant of the collection survived the move to 11 Chandos Street in 1873, and we have no catalogue of the museum.

Cataloguing of the library has been a recurrent trouble and expense to the Society. In 1788 Doctors Lettsom and Sims were requested to present plans. To save expense a written, rather than a printed, catalogue was made. Later, in October 1789, 250 copies of the catalogue were ordered to be printed. This was issued to every member in March 1790. At this time there were upwards of 10,000 volumes in the library, "many of them of singular rarity and value".

The library increased by the purchase of Dr. Sims' library in 1800 and by a large number of Lettsom's books in 1811 when he was compelled to raise money.

Dr. Henry Clutterbuck (see Ch. IV) was librarian from 1808–1815 and president in 1816. Throughout his membership he was devoted to the interests of the library, its arrangement and catalogue, but it was a time when the finances of the Society were in low water. There had been rows and dissension over the 21-year presidency of Dr. James Sims, which ended in the

Fig. 32. The title page of "Anatome corporis humani . . ." (*Venice, 1589*).

breakaway of members to form the Medico-Cirurgical Society. With them went many benefactions which, instead of being spent on the Society's library, went to build that of its rival.

In 1826 the Council invited voluntary subscriptions from members to reprint the catalogue of the library, which now contained 30,000 volumes. Clutterbuck's catalogue, inter-leaved, was published in 1829 and, with handwritten additions, remained in use until recent times.

In 1861 Dr. John Cockle was thanked and honoured by the Society for his work on the library. He verified and checked the catalogue and compiled a list of books that were missing. Over the first century of the Society's existence the number was great; but the library had been moved three times, and was then in George Street, Hanover Square, to which it had moved from Bolt Court in 1850.

In 1872 the Council decided that the proceedings of the Society should be published annually and from 1880–1940 these include a report from the Honorary Librarian. The Society was now more prosperous and its finances in a healthy state, and in 1873 the present home of the Society in Chandos Street was acquired. Again the library was moved by the long-suffering Dr. I. C. Thorowgood, Honorary Librarian 1872–1875.

When Mr. Royce Bell was librarian in 1880 money from the Fothergillian Trustees became available for improvement of the library. He rejoiced that "we will now be able to afford a collection of modern works, the one thing that was lacking to make our library what it ought to be". With the £50 from the Fothergillian Trust and more money from the Council a number of contemporary standard works on medicine, surgery and kindred sciences were added to the library, but in subsequent years it became increasingly difficult and expensive to carry out this policy as more text books were published and new editions followed one another. In 1883 an escape from this situation was offered by a subscription to Lewis's Medical Library.

There was general dissatisfaction and shame expressed by the Council in 1883 about the storage and inaccessibility of the books stored from basement to garret in the old house, but the Honorary Librarian promised that everything would be very satisfactory when the new building had been altered. In March 1884 "substantial new book cases had been provided on the walls of a suitable and commodious room". Yet Dr. Allchin reported gloomily that "fire, water and dust have wrought a disastrous effect upon the condition of many of the volumes". From 1882–1898 he and the Registrar, Mr. W. E. Poole, worked under great difficulty to get the library arranged and catalogued, during the building alterations, which continued for ten years. By 1886, 4,000 books dating from 1700 onwards were catalogued, but the older and most valuable part of the library remained to be done. At about this date the Council voted money for the cleaning and repair of the fifteenth and sixteenth-century books. In 1890, after 25 years' service to the library, Mr. Poole died, but Dr. Allchin carried on, with Mr. Hall to help him.

Money for the library was short and there were evidently long discussions whether to care for and repair the old books or to spend what money there was on buying new books to keep the library up to date.

In 1890 electric light was installed. The Royal Historical Society, whose books the Medical Society had been housing, removed them from the much-wanted shelves, but the Society had little money to devote to the library. The president, Sir James Crighton-Browne, made "a most handsome donation" to put the English medical works of the sixteenth and seventeenth centuries in a thoroughly satisfactory condition, and Mr. Hall, the Registrar, helped Dr. Allchin compile a card catalogue. Sir Richard Quain, Dr. Hughling Jackson and Sir William MacCormac (see Ch. IV) made useful donations for the repair of these old books.

Since 1895 the library committee has been required to keep a minute book for submission to the Council when required, so we know, for instance, that in spite of the library being open from 1.00.p.m. to 6.00.p.m. and Fellows permitted to borrow up to eight books, the library was then little used. In 1899 Dr.

Allchin, Honorary Librarian for 17 years, was presented with the Society's silver medal; became president in 1906 and continued to have the welfare of the library very much at heart.

Dr. Charles Daremberg, Professor of Medical History at the Sorbonne, had come from Paris in 1850 to examine the Greek manuscripts in our library which, no doubt, he used in his writings on the history of medicine. In 1903–4 Dr. Nias reported on the Greek manuscripts in the library showing that they were almost exclusively of Byzantine authorship. He praised them as being very fine specimens, well preserved though several bindings were in need of restoration. A world-wide interest in the library resulted from these reports.

In 1906, after a year of discussion and anxiety, the Society decided not to join in the amalgamation of other medical societies in London, but to maintain its independence; there is no doubt that the valuable library and premises which it owned made this decision possible and desirable.

To the Library Association meeting in 1914 the librarian, Mr. Bethell, was able to say that the library was kept well up-to-date with modern literature. A bequest by Lord Lister of 2,500 volumes had been catalogued and added to the library. In the twentieth century the problem of making new works available to Fellows was solved by increasing the subscription to Lewis's to 30 volumes.

During the 1914–18 War few books were bought and funds were prudently conserved, but about 1920 the library again became active. By 1924 the recataloguing of the seventeenth-century books was completed. Dr. Herbert Spencer, a former president, gave £50 for rebinding some of the seventeenth and eighteenth-century books. Dr. Arthur Voelcker, Honorary librarian from 1902–1934, gave the Society a fine bookcase for the then new reading room.

In 1926 and 1927 the twin problems which beset librarians, shelf space and accurate cataloguing, were raised, and the disposal of some duplicate copies was recommended. The main catalogue was 100 years old. A new catalogue would cost £450.

Through the generosity of the Honorary Librarian, Dr. Voelcker, and other Fellows the sum was raised, but this seems to have been spent chiefly on rebinding and cleaning some of the old books.

FIG. 33. Francis Arthur Voelcker (1861–1946). Librarian (*Royal College of Physicians*).

In 1928 the famous Ward Diaries were sold by auction. These 16 volumes had been acquired from the Society by Dr. James Sims, and consist of the jottings of a parson doctor from 1647–1673. In 1839 Dr. Severn, Registrar of the Society, had transcribed extracts, but it is to Sir D'Arcy Power (see Ch. IV) that the Society is indebted for a complete transcription and annotation made between 1913 and 1926. The books cannot rightly be called diaries; there are many blank pages and others so crowded with small writing that a glass must be used to read them.

The period of the Commonwealth and Restoration which the 16 volumes cover is an eventful one, and the friends and associates of Dr. Ward at Christchurch, Oxford and as vicar of Stratford-on-Avon add to their significance. Harvey was eight years his senior; and Willis, whom he so much admired and quoted, was eight years his junior; he was contemporary with Wren and Scarborough. The Royal Society was founded then, on the ruins of the defunct Commonwealth Society.

In 1662 Ward bought the vicarage of Stratford, after the Restoration, preferring the church to medicine; but for every page of sermons or theology there are ten of medical observations and speculation. As Sir D'Arcy says, Ward was more interested in the urine of his parishioners than in their spiritual state.

Perhaps the most interesting page is in Volume 2:

"What was the Teutonic Order?"
"Shakespear, Drayton and Ben Johnson had
"a merry meeting and it seems drank too hard
"for Shakespeare died of a fever thence contracted."
"Hares in winter time turn white all over Livonia".

Succession splash and draining of hydrothorax is well described as is "stroking" treatment of Lady Anne Conway at nearby Ragley Hall by the Irish quack Valentine Great-Strakers, and methods of embalming are also described.

Whether or not these diaries were of "Shakespearean rather than medical interest" they were sold in April 1928 for £10,500 to Dr. V. A. Rosenbach of New York (see Ch. VII). Most of the money was put towards buying the freehold of 11 Chandos Street and some was spent on repairs and rebinding of books in the library. A professional librarian, Mr. Egbert Smart, was also engaged to prepare a catalogue and card index, which was completed in 1932 and further extensive rebinding had been undertaken by Messrs. Fox. Mr. Haines Carter was responsible for many of the valuable rebindings.

No account of the library would be complete without tribute to Mr. Warren Dawson, F.R.C.S., who catalogued the 164 volumes of manuscripts from the fourteenth to nineteenth centuries. This catalogue was published in 1932 and its scholarship was admired both here and in America. The Greek manuscripts are thought to have come from the Askew Library and to have been bought by James Sims in 1722–onwards.

The Society acquired the greater number of these manuscripts when they purchased James Sims' books in 1801 (see also Ch. VII). They all bear Sims' signature and those added by Lettsom his (Lettsom's) book plate.

Dr. Arnold Chaplin made a valuable gift to the Society in 1936/37 of more than 360 engravings of medical men, and in thanking him the Council hoped that this would form the nucleus of a larger collection. A collection of portraits of past presidents of the Society was also nearly completed.

Interest in their illustrious founder was stimulated by the presentation to the Society of a volume entitled "Lettsom Relics 1768–1810", the gift of Mr. Hugh Elliot, Lettsom's great-grandson, while Dr. Johnston Abraham, librarian 1955 to 1963, with his well-illustrated "Life of Lettsom" (1933) provided a book of reference both for presidential addresses and for visiting lecturers.

During the war years only one volume of "Transactions" was published and economies were imperative. In November 1940 the library committee decided that all the most valuable books should be stored in the cellars. In spite of the conscientious efforts and care of the Registrar, Mr. Percy Minter, the condition of many bindings suffered from damp and mould but an unprecedented number of Fellows used the library in 1940 and 1941. In October 1942 the minute books, and 250 of the most valuable books, were temporarily dispersed and the only war casualties were some periodicals on their way to and from the printers. Through the untiring efforts of Dr. A. Hope Gosse, 11 students, and the Registrar, Mr. Minter, the library was restored to its pre-war state by 1946.

In the following years less use was made of the library by members of the Society and preservation was the chief care of the librarian and registrar. The subscription to Lewis's Library catered for the members needing current text books and the Society's library concentrated on medical history and biography.

At the meeting of the library committee in February 1964 the question of security was discussed. That any of the valuable books should be locked away in bank vaults was a negation of the library's purpose, for Lettsom's intention had been to provide "easy access to the best ancient and modern authors". It was therefore with relief and satisfaction that the librarian's suggestion to consult the Wellcome Historical Medical Museum was agreed to. The Wellcome Trust had in 1960 shown itself the friend of the Society and its library by contributing £800 to cover the cost of publishing an index of the "Transactions" from 1909–1959 (see Ch. VI). On behalf of the Wellcome Trustees Dr. Poynter, the Museum's Director, suggested that he and his expert librarians would house in the air-conditioned Wellcome Library any of the Society's books which they considered to be of exceptional merit and value. The conditions of this agreement include the cataloguing and insurance of the books deposited and which remain the sole property of the Society, under its name, and are available to members of the Society and to authorised readers. In November 1964 the Council readily approved these conditions and the agreement between the Society and the Trustees of Sir Henry Wellcome was signed on their behalf on July 4th, 1967. A very much larger number of books than was first anticipated by the Council was selected for deposit with the Wellcome Library; in fact more than 2,000, volumes and all the manuscripts.

The amenities of the Society's house, with the ceiling-high shelves of out-dated text books which were rarely used, still called for improvement. In 1967 the Council decided that many

Fig. 34. The title page of Hurtus Sanitatis (*Strassburg, 1491?*).

of them should be disposed of at the best possible price after Fellows had had the opportunity of acquiring any that they wanted. A number of books were possibly of value, but of general rather medical interest, such as an account of Roman Antiquities in Britain. It was decided that these should be submitted to sale by auction.

Since early in the Society's history it had been the policy to subscribe to, collect and bind periodicals, journals and the proceedings of other medical and kindred Societies. It became evident that the output of the printing presses was greater than the Society could afford or house. By 1965 the London teaching hospitals and medical centres had well-equipped up-to-date working libraries and the Council considered that better use could be made of the Society's limited funds, so agreed that £1,000 per annum should be saved by ceasing to subscribe to any periodicals other than the *Lancet* and the *British Medical Journal*.

Since 1967 the policy which should guide the Council in reforming the Society's library has been under discussion. The library will retain and collect books of biographical and historical medical interest, particularly those relating to our Founder or to various specialities. The books and manuscripts selected by the Wellcome Foundation and deposited in the safe keeping of their Historical Medical Library will be maintained and remain available to Fellows of the Society.

The Council consider that these changes are financially necessary and in keeping with our Founder's wishes under the different conditions of medical practice 200 years later. Our "Transactions" show that the Medical Society of London is not, and has no wish to be, a Society of medical history only but, as our Founder intended, exists to provide a forum for instruction and friendly discussion of the present and future trends of all branches of medicine and surgery today.

Acknowledgment

In writing this short account of the Society's Library I have drawn freely on the work of Miss Finola Hickey, a student of the College of Librarianship of Wales, and I acknowledge with thanks my debt to her for her research into our archives.

Lettsom's Letters

In February 1970 the Society was offered to purchase on favourable terms a packet of Letters and Correspondence of Dr. Lettsom which had come on to the market in London for which Yale University was bidding. These letters were inspected by the librarian and Dr. Poynter. The Council considered that they should be acquired by the Society and they were bought and are now in safe keeping.

The nature and interest of this miscellaneous collection of letters is difficult to convey but each gives a gleam of light on a facet of the busy life of Dr. Lettsom in his historical and social setting. Some are simply refusals and acceptances of invitations to dinner and social occasions, but there is an impressive number of long and intimate letters to and from doctors and professors in America, some of whom were founding members of now famous academic institutes and libraries. One of these is Dr. Benjamin Rush (1745–1813) (see "America" Ch. III) who writes to "My dear old Friend" to introduce the bearer; "the son of a respectable and opulent (Quaker) merchant" of Philadelphia. Dr. Rush was a physician and the first Professor of Chemistry at Philadelphia. He shared Lettsom's missionary zeal for the abolition of slavery and other humanitarian causes. His signature occurs in the Declaration of Independence. These two doctors interchanged "packets" of their publications and essays. Dr. John Warren of Boston, a former student of Sir Astley Cooper, writes in June 1815 to regret that "the unfortunate war between your country and ours has broken off intercourse I formerly enjoyed with you". By Dr. Codman, whom he commends to Lettsom for his good qualities, he sends a "packet" for the library of the Medical Society of London. At Harvard, where he was Professor of Anatomy and Surgery in 1847, there now stands the Warren Museum.

Dr. Jedidiah Morse (1761–1826), a congregational clergy-

man described as "the Father of American Geography" writes
to "My worthy and respected friend" in October 1812, thanking him warmly for his kindness to his son Samuel who he had
sent to London to study painting. He was secretary of the
Society for the Propagation of the Gospel among Indians and
author of many geographical works, but Sam's eponymous
fame eclipses his father's invention of Morse Telegraphy.

Thoroughly business-like documents of loans of money to
scientific authors form a part of the collection. There is an
indenture and a Deed of Covenant with William Curtis,
apothecary, for a loan of £500 by Dr. Lettsom to help the
publication of "Flora Londinensis" in 1786. David Ramsey of
Charleston was writing a "History of South Carolina in 1808"
and writes a grateful letter saying he is drawing on Dr. Lettsom
to pay the printers in New York.

It is to be regretted that we do not have Lettsom's replies to
several long letters about patients from provincial doctors
seeking his opinion in consultation. There are, for example,
long and very friendly letters from Dr. Struve, who encloses
his silhouette, on the results of treatment of smallpox. Dr.
Vaughan of Leicester describes the progress of a case of rabies,
and Dr. Wilmer of Coventry details the treatment and observes
the fatal termination of a patient with carcinoma of the
oesophagus.

Dr. Lettsom's wide interest in humanitarian causes is
reflected in a long letter from Dr. Jonathan Stokes of
Chesterfield. He writes as a good Quaker distressed by harsh
application of the Poor Laws suggesting how to relieve unem-
ployment, which was the cause of destitution in rural areas of
England in 1816. He urges plans for employing the poor in the
reclamation of farmland by clearing furze and bracken, and
fencing roads (but leaving sufficient cover for game birds which
he details). His idea on shortening the courses of rivers and
streams by straightening them would hardly have commended
itself to the farmers.

In some letters Lettsom's piety, good nature and sound
sense are wrapped in metaphor and quotation. The long letter

to his intimate friend, Dr. Pettigrew (see Ch. IV) could not be written today. At a meeting of the Society in June 1813 there had been an explosion of ill temper between Dr. Goode and Dr. Brown. Lettsom undertakes to soothe Goode and urges Pettigrew to "coalesce in cordiality" with Brown and all are invited to coffee in Sambrook Court at "seven precisely to shake hands like philosophers and fellow labourers in a noble Society". In Lettsom's letter of sympathy to Lady Erskine on the death of her friend the Countess of Huntingdon his deeply religious nature finds expression in devout, carefully penned Quaker sentences. A letter of August 10th, 1791 to Dr. Thornton in Philadelphia is in quite another mood. Lettsom is replying to a letter "of such turbulent politics that the ocean would become rough where the letters crossed" and his adverse criticism of Pitt may sound strange to modern ears, as do some of his economic views. "I think as meanly of Pitt as thou dost, and his whole political career has born(e) the aspect of a noisy orator with a superficial head that is great in cunning and little in great national concerns ... I consider him a worse minister than Lord North was". The long letter expresses his confidence that Lord Shelburne was wrong in saying that when we lost America "the sun of England was set forever". He has faith in democracy and Free Trade. "A mercantile nation surrounded with water, a hilly country or a cold one will ever be free, a warm valley with luxuriant soil will tend to slavery and despotism".

Dr. James Sims (1741–1820); is rightly regarded by the historians of the Society as the despot of 22 early years, but he remained a close friend of Lettsom—"the oldest friend I believe I have in London". There are two rather pathetic letters of February 1816 from the old arthritic doctor in Bath where "I am turned almost a hermit". He is alone and busy reading and writing in the great cold (the thermometer had been at 13°, he says) and revising his chemical paper "to be read to the Philosophical Society and correcting proofs". He warns his friends to expect flood and plague in London when summer comes, as had happened after the great frost of 1740.

This mixed bag of correspondence provides a revealing sidelight on our Founder, occupied as he is with many and diverse humanitarian and medical projects in London, the countryside and America. One wonders how he can have found time to meet the demands which his busy practice made on him.

Reference

Severn, Charles. Diary of the Rev. John Ward H.M. (from 1648–1678) arranged by Charles Severn. London. Henry Colburn 1839.

Chapter VI

"Transactions" of the Society

CUTHBERT E. DUKES

The first published records of the Society appeared under the title of "Memoirs" or "Proceedings" and owed much to the successful "Medical Transactions" published a little earlier (1767) by the Royal College of Physicians. Under one or other of these headings there still exist volumes covering the years 1787–1805 and 1810–1817; it seems to have been thanks to Lettsom's energy that after the dispute with Dr. Sims over the presidency and a lapse in records, the "Transactions" were revived and continued by Dr. Thomas Walshman, who had been in general practice in Southwark and succeeded in doubling attendance at the Society's meetings.

Subsequent volumes appeared only in 1846, 1861 and 1862. In 1872 regular annual publication was resumed under the title "Transactions", and these have appeared annually since that date; the year 1972, bicentenary of the Society, is thus also centenary of the "Transactions".

For more than fifty years it was the duty of one of the Honorary Secretaries of the Society to edit records. No doubt they varied in their editorial experience and possibly also in the punctuality of their performance. To overcome this Council decided in 1926 to appoint one Fellow as Honorary Secretary of the "Transactions", in which office he could continue for a period of years. The first to be so appointed was Thomas Percy Legg, who served from 1926–1930, when he died unexpectedly at the age of 58. Legg is also recorded in the official list of our benefactors, having left the Society a legacy of £1,000, although this was not actually received until the end of World War II. During the war years publication of the "Transactions" had been temporarily suspended for reasons of economy, and the legacy contributed to the cost of an enlarged Volume 63, named by the Council the "Legg Memorial Volume".

The first index to the "Transactions" was compiled by John Langton and covered the first 31 volumes issued between 1872 and 1908. Langton undertook all this clerical work single-handed, and it was only when his self-imposed labour was almost complete that he informed the Council and offered it as a gift to the Society. Sad to record, he died while the index was still in the press, and it was published the following year (1931). Langton was convinced that these first volumes contained valuable contributions to medical science, and that the "Transactions" were rather "in the condition of an unworked mine which needed my systematic labour to make its buried treasures available for the common good."

During my period of office as editor I decided that the "unworked mine" needed to be explored again, and that it would be useful to compile a second index of the "Transactions" covering the years 1909–1959 (volumes 32–75 inclusive). I asked permission of the Council to undertake this on the understanding that it would not involve the Society in any expense, and my suggestion was gratefully approved. I then approached the Wellcome Trust and received the promise of a generous grant of up to £800 to cover the costs of printing a second index, to be distributed free to all Fellows of the Society and to many libraries throughout the world.

The initial clerical worked involved in compiling this index was begun by a former Registrar, the late Mr. Percy Minter, and was completed by his successor Lt. Col. E. J. Tucker, with the help of Mr. John Leaney. It was my duty as editor of the "Transactions" to direct and supervise this work, and the second index was completed in February 1961.

Honorary Editors of the Transactions

T. P. Legg	1926–1930
E. P. Gould	1931–1939
W. E. Tanner	1940–1951
C. E. Dukes	1951–1962
A. Willcox	1962–1963
E. M. Jepson	1964–

Chapter VII

Finances of the Society

E. Maxwell Ellis

Our Society's unbroken existence for two hundred years undoubtedly owes much to its financial structure. Fortunate in the early years, successive Councils later managed the finances with such skill and courage that we celebrate our bicentenary with an unlimited potential for survival. Our sound finances date from the initial recognition that a permanent home for the Society was essential, and the possession of its own premises has been the constant concern of successive Councils.

Crane Court, 1774

At first meetings were held either at the houses of members or at coffee shops, but within six months of its foundation the Society took the lease of a house at Crane Court, at a rent of £40 a year, in the name of Dr. John Millar, the first president (see Ch. IV). Later, Lettsom and four other members personally indemnified Millar against loss and took over the lease and keys. The possession of a house brought responsibility for land tax, window tax, sewer, tythe, watch, poor and Church rates, varying slightly in amount, but always nearly £20 a year. There were also the expenses of repairs and decorations, and the initial costs of converting and furnishing the lower floor for the Society's purposes.

The income to cover these expenses was derived from a subscription of one guinea and an admission fee of three guineas, imposed in 1775. This amounted on average to about £80 a year. As the upper part of the house was not needed, it was let to a member named Pearce, a surgeon, for £15 a year free of tax, and, when he left in 1780, to another member and surgeon, Mr. Cumberledge, who paid thirty guineas a year inclusive. The total income proved inadequate, for besides the expenses of running its house, the Society constantly pursued one of its original aims of collecting a library and frequently bought

Fig. 35. The house used by the Medical Society in Crane Court (*Wellcome Trust*).

books. It incurred considerable bills for the printing of summonses and of dissertations, served refreshments at its frequent meetings, conducted a foreign correspondence, and subscribed to learned journals. In 1775, when the accounts were in debit

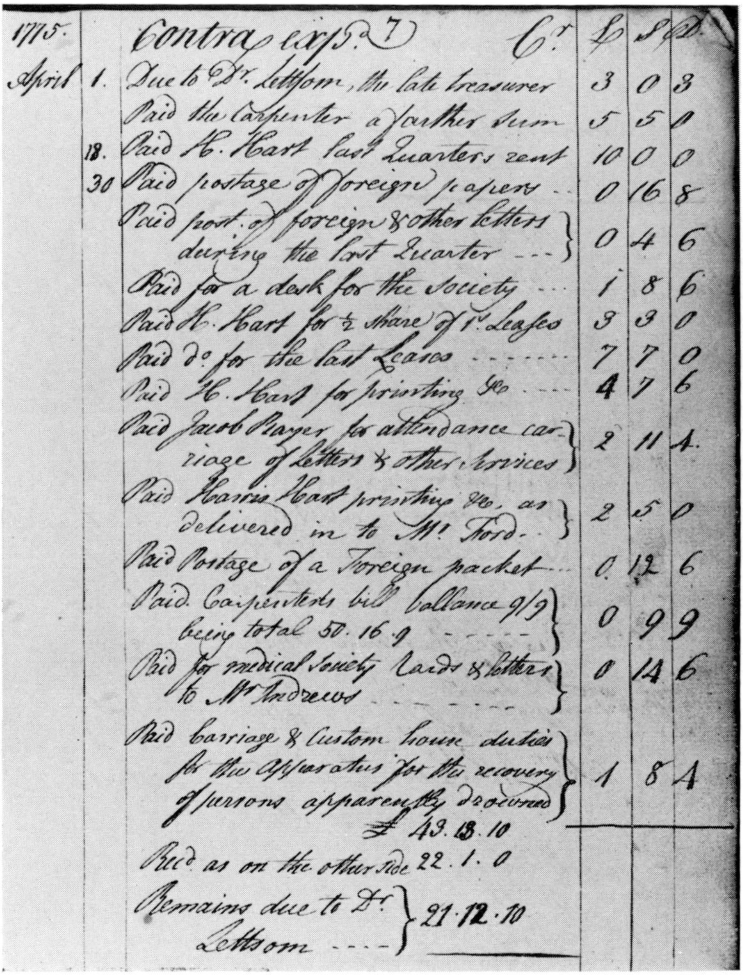

1775.		Contra exps. 7) Cr.	£	s	d
April	1.	Due to Dr. Lettsom, the late treasurer	3	0	3
		Paid the Carpenter a farther sum	5	5	0
	18.	Paid H. Hart last Quarters rent	10	0	0
	30	Paid postage of foreign papers ..	0	16	8
		Paid post. of foreign & other letters during the last Quarter ---	0	4	6
		Paid for a desk for the Society ...	1	8	6
		Paid H. Hart for ½ share of 1st Leases	3	3	0
		Paid do. for the last Leases ------	7	7	0
		Paid H. Hart for printing &c ---	4	7	6
		Paid Jacob Payer for attendance carriage of Letters & other Services	2	11	4
		Paid Harris Hart printing &c. as delivered in to Mr. Ford.	2	5	0
		Paid Postage of a Foreign packet...	0	12	6
		Paid Carpenters bill ballance 9/9 being total 50. 16. 9 -----	0	9	9
		Paid for medical Society Cards & letters to Mr Andrews -----	0	14	6
		Paid carriage & Custom house duties for the Apparatus for the recovery of persons apparently drowned	1	8	4
		£ 43. 18. 10			
		Recd as on the other side 22. 1. 0			
		Remains due to Dr. Lettsom --- 21. 12. 10			

FIG. 36. A page from the Society's accounts 1775, showing the payment of carriage and customs and duties for resuscitation apparatus.

to the treasurer, the Society pursued one of its interests, and paid £1.8.4. "for carriage and customs", (see "Royal Humane Society" in Ch. III) of "an apparatus for the recovery of persons apparently drowned".

Bolt Court, *1787*

Lettsom made no attempt to curb these activities and indeed possibly encouraged them, as it was his own style of living. At any rate he annually paid out of his own pocket for the overspending, and in 1787 gave the Society £100 to put it in balance, a gift noted by the Audit Committee as a "liberal donation".

In the same year he made an even more handsome gift, presenting the freehold of No. 3 Bolt Court, Fleet Street, to James Sims and Stephen Lowdall in trust for the Medical Society of London, with the proviso that the house was to revert to his own trustees if the membership fell below twenty for six months. Fortunately, this never happened, and the possession of a fine house, then valued at £2,500, containing a library capable of holding 40,000 books, proved a secure base on which to build a future. The Society endured vicissitudes of fortune thereafter, but having survived the secession in 1805 of some eminent members, over the dispute on Sims's repeated re-election as president, nothing seriously threatened the permanence ensured by the possession of its own home.

Two years after the move to Bolt Court the day-to-day finances were in a bad way. The move itself was expensive and upkeep, including increased taxes and rates, was higher than that of Crane Court. In the summer of 1789 some books were sold, including the copyright of the first volume of the "Memoirs", for £257.16.0, restoring a balance to the Society. To show its financial resilience, in the following year £100 of 3% Consols were purchased for £78, and further purchases were made from time to time when funds accumulated. As fortunes fell these securities were realised, and in 1811, during one of the crises of the Napoleonic wars, when the subscription income fell to £45, £200 of 3% Consols were sold for £127.10.0, a considerable loss on the book value. By 1813, matters had improved, and the Society insured its house with the Globe Insurance Company for £3,000. In 1818, funds again ran low and to pay for repairs to the house, two Fellows lent £30 each.

Fig. 37. The Medical Society's House in Bolt Court (*Wellcome Trust*).

In the following year "books, duplicates, etc." were sold for £128.1.6., enabling the Society to repay its members and again return to credit. Up to modern times, buying and selling books has always been an important activity in the Society's fluctuating fortunes (see Ch. V).

1800–1850

The Society steadily prospered during the first forty years of the last century. Membership remained high in numbers and quality, and by purchases and gifts the library increased rapidly in size and value. It was based on the purchase in 1801 of nearly 6,000 books from its then president, James Sims. He was paid £500 and later given an annuity of £15 a year. The capital sum is not recorded in the account book, although it was possibly the largest amount ever spent by a medical society in buying books from a private library.

Then times changed. Towards the middle of the century there was a noticeable drift to the West End of the well-to-do City inhabitants, followed by a similar migration of their physicians. This affected the membership and activities of the Society, as for several years up to 1850 income did not cover expenditure. It was thus obliged to join this movement or disappear.

In order to move and retain possession of Bolt Court, the permission of Lettsom's heirs was necessary, but they willingly resigned their contingent interest. It was more difficult to establish the Society's own claim on the house, as it was vested in trustees who had died. After a good deal of legal argument an order in Chancery was obtained allowing the Society to appoint three Trustees who signed a deed acknowledging the Society's interest in their Trust. This method has been followed ever since, and there are now four Trustees elected by the Council of the Society on death or resignation of an incumbent.

George Street, 1850

In 1850, the Society secured the lease of premises at 33 George Street, Hanover Square, for £100 a year, inclusive of

rates and taxes. At the same time it merged with the
Westminster Medical Society. In various histories of the
Medical Society of London it has been written that the

FIG. 38. An engraving of Hanover Square in 1787 (*British Museum*).

Westminster Medical Society was almost defunct at this time,
but the minutes of a Council Meeting on 12th April, 1850,
seem to indicate the reverse. At this meeting the finances of the
move were considered, and the conjoined Societies' income
was estimated at £260, made up of £52.10.0., from fifty subscribing members of the Medical Society of London, and
£157.10.0., from 150 subscribing members of the Westminster
Medical Society (and £50 for letting the house in Bolt Court).
It appears that the smaller society absorbed the larger, because
the latter had no fixed meeting place. Lettsom's gift of Bolt
Court thus preserved the identity of the Society in circum-
stances which would otherwise have ensured its demise.

11 Chandos Street, 1873

As the lease of the George Street rooms was due to expire in 1873 and as the landlord had given notice of intent to raise the rent, a search for a more suitable place was begun in 1870. Towards the latter part of 1872 Turner's house, 23 Queen Anne Street, came on the market but the price for the lease was too high. At the same time 11 Chandos Street was on offer by the Earl of Gainsborough at £150 a year for a 21-year repairing lease. The Council of the Society could not make up its mind, but the president, Thomas Bryant, acted with great determination and personally signed the lease for the Society when its Trustees refused. Considerable structural alteration were necessary, including raising one ceiling by fifteen feet for a meeting room. The liquid funds were £345 and a conservative estimate for the building work was £500, in addition to fees to the architect and solicitor, and furnishings (the final cost, of course, was far greater). The Trustees could not sell Bolt Court, but were persuaded to lend £500, the accumulated excess in the Fothergillian Fund, on the guarantee of three members of the Society. Thomas Bryant again came up to scratch as a guarantor.

The Society moved in April, 1873, but by October, after paying numerous bills, there was only £25.6.11., in the bank to meet an over-due instalment of £100 on the builder's account. The builder was asked to accept £50, to be paid the next day for the workmen's wages. The Treasurer was then requested to obtain a £50 loan from the Centenary Fund to pay the rest. This Fund, started in 1872 and closed in 1874, consisted of donations from the Fellows. Altogether, £158.6.0., was collected and spent on furnishings. A bank loan of £200 was obtained in March, 1874, to help pay the builder and architect.

The new premises had evidently not been properly surveyed for they were found to be in a poor state of repair. For years the Society spent considerable sums in renewing rebuilding and on one occasion reinforcing to keep out the rats. However, the house was commodious and attracted tenants, while as time passed more Fellows joined the Society, also attracted by the spacious surroundings. From the increased income the debts were slowly paid and by October, 1876, the Society was out of debt and in balance at the bank. It received nearly £400 a year from lettings, £50 a year from Bolt Court and there were 350 subscribing Fellows.

12 Chandos Street, 1881

At the end of 1881, No. 11A (now No. 12) Chandos Street came on offer. The Council were unafraid of the sums involved in a repairing lease of 60 years for the two properties at a rent of £300 a year, and an estimate of £4,000 for alterations, the lease to be granted on their completion. A bank loan of £500 was raised and Sir Erasmus Wilson (see Ch. IV) offered a temporary loan of £2,000 at 4% with which to begin the building work. Tenders were invited and the lowest of seven, £3,395, was accepted. When the lease was granted, a mortgage of £4,000 was raised on the two properties from the Briton Life Association. Sir Erasmus was repaid £2,200 with interest of £38.16.0. and the bankers, Sir Samuel Scott & Co., were repaid £500 and £4.6.3. interest.

House and Finance Committee

The handling of these large sums of money was now placed in the hands of a House and Finance Committee which was formed by the Council and met for the first time on 14th March, 1884. Later that year forms for the payment of subscriptions by a banker's order were sent to Fellows. Hitherto the subscriptions had been collected by the Registrar and later by a professional collector, both paid 5% on moneys collected. The collector continued to receive this percentage for some time after the innovation of banker's orders.

As considerable sums were still necessary for building work and producing the "Transactions", the House and Finance Committee proposed an issue of 40 Debenture Bonds each of £100 nominal, to be offered at £97, bearing 4% interest, and repayment to be by drawing from time to time. These were all taken up by Fellows and the Society cleared its mortgage debt and bank loan. It was calculated that the excess of income over estimated expenditure would suffice to redeem these bonds in about fifteen years.

FIG. 39. An engraving of Cavendish Square in 1800 (*British Museum*).

Extensions to 11 & 12 Chandos Street, 1892

A Mr. Gabriel had become the freeholder of 11 and 12 Chandos Street and offered to negotiate the freehold with the Society, suggesting as a credit point that they could build over the garden. The price was considered excessive and the Society discontinued the negotiations. The freeholder then arranged with a builder, Mr. Boyce, to build in the garden space, providing he could secure from the Society some of their frontage to Chandos Street and permission to extend their ground floor, some of which area would then belong to the Society. If a scheme satisfactory to Mr. Gabriel could be agreed, the Society's lease would be replaced by another at the same rent for the larger premises the Society would acquire. All this was covered by legal agreements. During Mr. Boyce's building the Society itself initiated some internal alterations including more cellar space, and found it necessary to re-roof the library and repair the rest of the roof. It also took the opportunity to refurnish most of the premises. Hot water pipe heating was proposed but abandoned because of the extra cost.

By 1895 the Society owed £3,100 to Debenture holders and the bank, but from its enlarged premises and expanding membership a £300 surplus of income over expenditure could be foreseen. Therefore a further issue of £1,500 of Debenture Bonds, making £3,600 in all, was made and rapidly taken up by the Fellows. The Bonds were to be redeemed by the end of 1907.

At some stage after the building works were finished, the freeholder refused to grant the Society the new lease agreed between them. Mr. Boyce also came into this quarrel which was taken to law and hung in the Courts until a final judgment was given in the Society's favour on the 12th November, 1902, when the new lease was executed with 39 years to run. The Judge ruled, however, that the Society was responsible for most of the costs which came to £1,083. Part of this was met out of income and £750 borrowed from the bank to complete payment. This loan was repaid in two years.

Sale of Bolt Court, 1915

The Society's finances slowly and steadily improved, but considerable sums were spent on the House, while the Bolt Court property was becoming more and more dilapidated. Advice to get rid of it was accepted by the Trustees and it was sold in 1915 for £1,357, its book value being £2,500 in 1787. The money was invested for the Society in the names of the Charity Commissioners and yielded an interest of about £60 a year against the £80 or so obtained by letting it. The Society saved more than this on the cost of repairs.

Freehold of 11 & 12 Chandos Street, 1928

During the 1914 war the income dropped a good deal and by 1919 the current finances were at a low ebb. It was decided to raise the subscription, unchanged since the founding of the Society in 1773, from one guinea to two guineas a year. This had the immediate effect of restoring useful credit balances. In 1921, Dr. Lloyd Roberts left the Society £2,200 with which the then remaining £1,800 of Debenture Bonds were redeemed.

The business handled by the House and Finance Committee and the financial responsibility shouldered by the Honorary Treasurer and the Registrar were now considerable. To lighten these burdens the Committee suggested the engagement of a professional auditor and the accounts for the year ending 30th September, 1926, were for the first time presented over the signature of a chartered accountant. The weight of the financial transactions since then has increased regularly and it would now be unthinkable to deal with them in any other way.

In this same year, 1926, the Society was relieved of the burden of income tax at the instance of the Charity Commissioners. The Registrar of Friendly Societies had in 1905 procured an exemption from certain local rates and taxes and in 1906 from the then existing Corporation tax.

When the opportunity came in 1928 to acquire the freehold of the property, the Society as a thriving body was well poised to enter into negotiations. The House and Finance Committee were in no doubt on the desirability of this action and Council agreed to the sale at Sotheby's of the James Ward Diaries (see Ch. V). These 16 volumes fetched £10,000 clear of expenses and with £2,000 borrowed from the Westminster Bank (as Sir Samuel Scott's bank had now become) the freehold was bought from Mrs. Gabriel. The property is in the books at £16,000, but its current value must be very much greater. The sound advice of the House and Finance Committee was amply justified by this wonderful purchase and by the record on the 27th March, 1931, that the Society was free of all debt.

1930–1939

Throughout the thirties the Society continued to save and invest. A thriving organisation is always supported, and many legacies and gifts were received. As the Society was now completely solvent, the surplus money was regularly invested, unfortunately largely in Government stocks, as then directed by statute. The capital value has seriously declined. The proceeds of the sale of Bolt Court and those of the substantial Stubber legacy (received in 1926) had been rather unnecessarily segregated into separate funds. In 1936, they were coalesced under the non-eponymous title of General Investments.

1939–1970

After the war the total investments amounted to over £10,000 and two important subsidiary funds were established to fill special needs.

Pension Fund. The Society's Registrar is an ancient office, dating from the resident factotum in Crane Court. The retirement of successive Registrars invariably posed the question of a pension or an honorarium which the Society at that particular time could often ill afford. Shortly after the last war an Endowment Annuity Insurance policy was acquired to deal with this responsibility and in 1952 the policy was surrendered and a Pension Fund established with the proceeds.

Building Fund. In 1962 a Building Fund was formed into which money was channelled from time to time as funds accumulated. Both these funds have amply justified their creation.

After the 1939–45 war the House was in poor condition from war damage (it was badly blasted in 1940) and from inevitable and enforced neglect, but it was impossible to obtain the necessary building licences to do more than repair the major defects. An old building not properly and uniformly heated always runs a risk of harbouring wood rot. This came to light in 1968, and a formidable building operation was necessary to remedy the damage at a cost of over £10,000. The invested funds were fortunately adequate to meet this disaster, but only just.

Bicentenary renovations. As these works were being finished, Council decided that a complete renovation of the building was necessary and should be completed before 1973, the bicentenary year. Sufficient liquid funds were not available, but in the transfer of some of the more valuable books to the Wellcome Institute many duplicate books were found and others of value but not in the context of the Society's aims (see Ch. V). These books were sold and part of the money used for the work of renovation to be completed in time for the bicentenary week in May 1973. The remainder has been invested and again the Society is prosperous; the Founder would have relished the acumen his successors have shown in building on the practical foundation he laid by his priceless gift of Bolt Court.

The Society has had a reputation for conservatism, for which little reason can be found. The reputation could not have derived from the professional meetings, where no current medical trend ever failed to attract discussion. The financial operations of successive Councils were nearly always far-sighted and sometimes bold to the verge of rashness. Finally, the imputation of conservatism can hardly be supported by the following pioneering activities:

1883   Hot air or hot water pipe heating proposed. Not installed due to lack of funds.

1890   Electric lighting installed.

1903   Telephone installed.

1907   Typewriter acquired.

1909   Gas geyser hot water supply installed.

1913   Vacuum cleaner bought.

We truly stand on the shoulders of our predecessors.

Appendix—Special Funds

Fothergillian Fund

An early member, Anthony Fothergill, when he died in 1813, left a legacy of £500 to the Society for the provision of medals. It was decided to use this for a gold medal to replace one given on six occasions by Lettsom in memory of John Fothergill, but not awarded for eight years. The legacy was not finally made over until 1822, when it was invested. In 1825, a separate account was established, the Fothergillian Fund, used only for gold medals and sometimes for library purposes. As gold medals were not awarded unless papers of sufficient merit were offered, and as they are now given triennially, the Fund gradually accumulated money and by 1963 had a book value of £916 in 2½% Consols. The capital was clearly undergoing a rapid erosion and it was decided to cut the loss. The Official Trustees of Charitable Trusts, to whom the fund had been transferred in 1891, agreed and sold the stock for £394.10.0. which was re-invested in £410 worth of shares in The Charities Official Investment Fund.

Gant Bequest

In 1906 Mrs. Gant left the Society £101.18.11, in memory of her husband, as a Fund, the interest from which was to be used for the Library.

Lloyd Roberts Lecture

In 1921 Dr. Lloyd Roberts left £500 to endow a lecture to be given annually and arranged in succession by the Medical Society of London, the Royal College of Physicians and the Royal Society of Medicine. The Fund is vested in the Trustees of the Medical Society of London.

Chapter VIII

The Bicentenary and the Society's Future

R. D. TONKIN

The first meeting of the Medical Society of London was held in May 1773, and Council decided that the two hundredth anniversary should be commemorated firstly by making some

FIG. 40. 1971: the Library at 11 Chandos Street, before alterations.

major changes in the Society's house and secondly by holding some special celebrations in May 1973.

The reconstruction and renovation of the Meeting Room, library, hall, cloakrooms and exterior at 11 Chandos Street, renamed Lettsom House, involved building work lasting over

Fig. 41. 1972: the old Library (Fellows' Room) after alterations.

two years, but brought back much of the graceful Regency style and decoration which it had partly lost. The social events planned include an open week at Lettsom House with exhibits of the Founder, publication of the history of the Society, a special anniversary dinner, and a reception and Oration to be held at the Royal College of Physicians by the kindness of the President. The suggestion that members might make a pilgrimage to Lettsom's birthplace in Tortola could not be adopted.

When the Medical Society first occupied 11 Chandos Street it housed for some years the Royal Historical Society, and has continued to provide accommodation for other Societies since then. A close link with the Harveian Society has existed for many years, and the new facilities arising from its bicentenary modernisation offer further opportunities for providing hospitality. A centre close to Harley Street where informal groups can meet and where lectures or committees can be held, is likely to be of increasing value and it will be possible to provide some form of catering, either for small private gatherings or for society meetings.

The purpose of the Medical Society of London is to be found in its first law:

> "The Medical Society of London, founded in 1773, has for its objectives the Advancement of the Science of Medicine and Surgery Exclusively."

and this remains its primary objective.

During the last decade, due largely to heavier demands upon members' time the progressive multiplication of scientific conferences, symposia, teach-ins etc., and above all the steady worsening of traffic congestion in London, attendance at meetings has declined. Though this decline does not imply a serious loss of interest in the Society, its present position demands critical thought and a flexible approach towards future development.

The furtherance of the science of medicine involves far more than the regular presentation of papers by appropriate experts, as the format of our own meetings has always recognised— subsequent discussion from the floor has always been regarded as an essential contribution. The now familiar panel symposium is an extension of this, but it is conceivable that more intimate and personal discussions could be organised within the framework of a society such as ours.

Subject matter might also be broadened to include other subjects relevant to medicine, such as community organisation, educational planning, international problems and even moonwalking, with various experts in these fields invited to discuss their subjects with us. Accounts of various expeditions and even, occasionally, personal travel experiences could prove valuable, besides possibly lending a little more emphasis to entertainment.

Greater consideration might be given to more frequent joint meetings with our sister societies, such as the Harveian, the Osler Club, Chelsea Clinical, etc., and invitations extended to some of the newer postgraduate organisations outside London.

Important as such meetings are, the spread of medical knowledge depends greatly upon conversation between people, for which frequent, and not necessarily formal, gatherings of individuals or groups are essential. In these frenetic and expensive days both clubs and specialist societies are finding their survival threatened, but by offering Fellows some of the facilities of a club the Society may well help to achieve its primary and traditional objectives. With this in mind, the old library has been transformed into a less formal, but more comfortable and welcoming centrally-heated Fellows' Room.

In a preceding chapter Mr. Woodd-Walker has given an account of the history of our library. He explains how it had become far too valuable in both academic and material senses, to be allowed to lie fallow, inaccessible to others, and inadequately protected. This problem has fortunately been solved through the good offices of the Wellcome Foundation, who have kindly agreed to take over a large number of the more valuable books on a twenty-year loan. These have been fully catalogued, housed in a controlled environment, and are now available to a wide range of scholars for reference and study.

The "treasures" having been safely housed we were left with many books, the majority of which were important and valuable, yet not of exclusive interest to our Fellows, many being in Latin and on subjects other than medicine. The Council decided to offer these for sale and to use the proceeds to defray the unforeseen yet inescapable expense of restoring the fabric of our Society's house, alarmingly damaged by the ravages of dry rot. It was also felt that the opportunity of the bicentenary should be taken to improve the facilities and appearance both inside and outside the building.

In 1971, some 2,000 volumes were bought—prior to sale at Sotheby's—by Dr. J. A. Hannah of Toronto, Ontario, for the purpose of founding an Institute of Medical History in Canada. This fine act of philanthropy, besides saving the books from being scattered at an auction sale, means that the Society's Library will in part continue its life in a new world and provide a continuing association between our 200-year old Society and the young and growing medical world of Canada.

We were then left with the decision as to what should be done for the future; that we should be without any library was unthinkable, since no human habitation, let alone an academic institution, can be considered civilised without books on its shelves. On the other hand both space and finance preclude any idea of building up a comprehensive medical reference library.

We still have in our possession a fair number of works of medical history and biography, and it was felt that this nucleus might well form the basis for future acquisitions in these two fields, particularly medical biography. A representative collection of up-to-date medical books and recent monographs could provide a modest but adequate nucleus for incidental reference, in addition to the standard directories available for essential information. With these might be a limited selection of journals such as the *British Medical Journal* and *Lancet* and perhaps some others of general as well as medical interest.

Finally, a start has been made on exploring the potentialities of audio-visual means of storing and disseminating technical information.

The Presidents of the Society

1773. JOHN MILLAR, M.D.
1775. JOHN COAKLEY LETTSOM, M.D., F.R.S.
1776. NATHANIEL HULME, M.D., F.R.S.
1779. GEORGE EDWARDS, M.D.
1780. SAMUEL FOART SIMMONS, M.D., F.R.S.
1783. JOHN SIMS, M.D.
1784. JOHN WHITEHEAD, M.D.
1785. JOHN RELPH, M.D.
1786. JAMES SIMS, M.D.*
1809. JOHN COAKLEY LETTSOM, M.D., F.R.S.
1811. GEORGE PINCKARD, M.D.
1813. JOHN COAKLEY LETTSOM, M.D., F.R.S.
1815. JOSEPH ADAMS, M.D.
1817. THOMAS WALSHMAN, M.D.
1819. HENRY CLUTTERBUCK, M.D.
1821. DAVID UNWINS, M.D.
1823. WILLIAM SHEARMAN, M.D.
1825. HENRY CLUTTERBUCK, M.D.
1827. JOHN HASLAM, M.D.
1829. THOMAS CALLAWAY
1831. JOHN BURNE, M.D.
1833. WILLIAM KINGDON.
1835. JOHN WHITING, M.D.
1837. THOMAS EGERTON BRYANT.
1839. LEONARD STEWART, M.D.
1840. HENRY CLUTTERBUCK, M.D.
1842. GEORGE PILCHER.
1844. THEOPHILUS THOMPSON, M.D., F.R.S.
1846. WALTER COOPER DENDY.
1848. HENRY HANCOCK.
1850. JAMES RISDON BENNETT, M.D.
1851. EDWARD WILLIAM MURPHY, M.D.
1852. JOHN BISHOP, F.R.S.
1853. FORBES WINSLOW, M.D., D.C.L.
1854. EDWARD HEADLAND.
1855. JOHN SNOW, M.D.
1856. WILLIAM DINGLE CHOWNE, M.D.
1857. FRANCIS HIRD
1858. WILLIAM HUGHES WILLSHIRE, M.D.

* *Dr. James Sims was President for twenty-one years.*

1859. JOHN HILTON, F.R.S.
1860. ALFRED BARING GARROD, M.D., F.R.S.
1861. WILLIAM COULSON.
1862. FRANCIS SIBSON, M.D., F.R.S.
1863. EDWIN CANTON.
1864. ROBERT GREENHALGH, M.D.
1865. ISAAC BAKER BROWN.
1866. CHARLES JOHN HARE, M.D.
1867. HENRY SMITH.
1868. BENJAMIN WARD RICHARDSON, M.D., F.R.S.
1869. PETER MARSHALL.
1870. JOHN GAY.
1871. ANDREW CLARK, M.D.
1872. THOMAS BRYANT.
1873. SAMUEL OSBORNE HABERSHON, M.D.
1874. VICTOR DE MÉRIC.
1875. CHARLES H. F. ROUTH, M.D.
1876. WILLIAM ADAMS.
1877. GEORGE BUCHANAN, M.D.
1878. ERASMUS WILSON, F.R.S.
1879. JOHN COCKLE, M.D.
1880. FREDERICK JAMES GANT.
1881. WILLIAM HENRY BROADBENT, M.D.
1882. FRANCIS MASON.
1883. Sir JOSEPH FAYRER, K.C.S.I., M.D., F.R.S.
1884. ARTHUR EDWARD DURHAM.
1885. WILLIAM M. ORD, M.D.
1886. ROBERT BRUDENELL CARTER.
1887. J. HUGHLINGS JACKSON, M.D., F.R.S.
1888. Sir WILLIAM MacCORMAC
1889. CHARLES THEODORE WILLIAMS, M.D.
1890. JOHN KNOWSLEY THORNTON.
1891. RICHARD DOUGLAS POWELL, M.D.
1892. JONATHAN HUTCHINSON, F.R.S.
1893. JOHN SYER BRISTOWE, M.D., F.R.S.
1894. Sir WILLIAM B. DALBY.
1895. Sir JAMES CRICHTON-BROWNE, M.D., F.R.S.
1896. REGINALD HARRISON.
1897. ARTHUR ERNEST SANSOM, M.D.
1898. EDMUND OWEN.
1899. FREDERICK T. ROBERTS, M.D.
1900. JOHN H. MORGAN, C.V.O.
1901. WILLIAM HENRY ALLCHIN, M.D.
1902. ALFRED PEARCE GOULD, M.S.
1903. F. DE HAVILLAND HALL, M.D.
1904. JOHN LANGTON.
1905. Sir LAUDER BRUNTON, M.D., F.R.S.
1906. CHARLES A. BALLANCE, M.V.O., M.S.
1907. JAMES KINGSTON FOWLER, M.D.

1908. CHARLES BARRETT LOCKWOOD.
1909. SAMUEL WEST, M.D.
1910. CHARTERS J. SYMONDS, C.B., M.S.
1911. J. MITCHELL BRUCE, C.V.O., M.D., LL.D.
1912. Sir W. WATSON CHEYNE, Bart., K.C.M.G., C.B., F.R.S.
1913. Sir DAVID FERRIER, M.D., F.R.S.
1914. JOHN BLAND SUTTON.
1915. WILLIAM PASTEUR, M.D.
1916. D'ARCY POWER.
1917. Sir StCLAIR THOMSON, M.D.
1918. ARTHUR FRANCIS VOELCKER, M.D.
1919. V. WARREN LOW, C.B.
1920. Sir WILLIAM HALE-WHITE, K.B.E., M.D.
1921. Sir JAMES BERRY, B.S.
1922. Lord DAWSON OF PENN, G.C.V.O., K.C.B., M.D.
1923. HERBERT R. SPENCER, M.D.
1924. EUSTACE M. CALLENDER, C.B.E., M.D.
1925. Sir HOLBURT J. WARING, M.S.
1926. Sir HUMPHRY ROLLESTON, Bart., K.C.B., M.D.
1927. HERBERT WILLIAM CARSON.
1928. JOHN WALTER CARR, C.B.E., M.D.
1929. DONALD J. ARMOUR, C.M.G.
1930. ROBERT ARTHUR YOUNG, C.B.E., M.D.
1931. HERBERT TILLEY, M.D.
1932. Sir JOHN F. H. BROADBENT, Bart., M.D.
1933. Sir JOHN THOMSON-WALKER, O.B.E.
1934. The Rt. Hon. The LORD HORDER, K.C.V.O., M.D.
1935. Professor GEORGE E. GASK, C.M.G., D.S.O.
1936. Sir WILLIAM WILLCOX, K.C.I.E., C.B., C.M.G., M.D.
1937. J. E. H. ROBERTS, O.B.E.
1938. CHARLES ERNEST LAKIN, M.D.
1939. VINCENT ZACHARY COPE, M.D., M.S.
1940. GORDON WILKINSON GOODHART, M.D.
1941. GORDON GORDON-TAYLOR, C.B., O.B.E., M.S.
1942. A. HOPE GOSSE, M.D.
1943. G. GREY TURNER D.Ch.
1944. ANTHONY FEILING, M.D.
1945. Sir JAMES WALTON, K.C.V.O., M.S.
1946. Sir PHILIP MANSON-BAHR, C.M.G., D.S.O., M.D.
1947. WILLIAM EDWARD TANNER, M.S.
1948. THEO. JENNER HOSKIN, M.D.
1949. LIONEL E. C. NORBURY, O.B.E.
1950. ARTHUR HENRY DOUTHWAITE, M.D.
1951. ALEXANDER CROYDON PALMER, O.B.E.
1952. CUTHBERT E. DUKES, O.B.E., M.D., M.Sc.
1953. ERIC WILLIAM RICHES, *M.C.*, M.S.
1954. Sir HORACE EVANS, G.C.V.O., M.D.
1955. ARTHUR DICKSON WRIGHT, M.S.
1956. THOMAS CECIL HUNT, D.M.

1957. Sir CECIL WAKELEY, Bt., K.B.E., C.B., LL.D., D.Sc.
1958. EDWARD REVILL CULLINAN, M.D.
1959. RONALD COVE-SMITH.
1960. NILS L. ECKHOFF, M.S.
1961. WILFRID GEORGE OAKLEY, M.D.
1962. EDWARD G. MUIR, M.S.
1963. ALEC L. WINGFIELD, M.D.
1964. GUY BLACKBURN, M.B.E., M.Chir.
1965. Sir RONALD BODLEY SCOTT, K.C.V.O., D.M.
1966. HENRY R. THOMPSON.
1967. Lt.-Gen. Sir ROBERT DREW, K.C.B., C.B.E.
1968. The Rt. Hon. the LORD BROCK, M.S.
1969. JOSEPH SMART, M.D.
1970. MAXWELL P. ELLIS, M.D., M.S.
1971. J. B. HARMAN, M.D.
1972. Sir HEDLEY ATKINS, K.B.E., D.M., M.Ch.

Benefactors of the Society

1773. JOHN COAKLEY LETTSOM, M.D., F.R.S.
1807. NATHANIEL HULME, M.D., F.R.S.
1814. ANTHONY FOTHERGILL, M.D., F.R.S.
1820. JAMES SIMS, M.D.
1842. JOHN LETTSOM ELLIOTT.
1887. PEDRO F. DE COSTA ALVARENGA.
1890. CHARLES THEODORE WILLIAMS, M.D.
1898. ROBERT BARNES, M.D.
1906. MRS. F. J. GANT.
1910. JOHN LANGTON.
1920. DAVID LLOYD ROBERTS, M.D., F.R.S.E.
1926. MISS O. H. STUBBER.
1933. JOHN HUGH ARMSTRONG ELLIOT.
1934. MRS. MARY J. WILLIAMS.
1937. ARNOLD CHAPLIN, M.D.
1942. HERBERT RITCHIE SPENCER, M.D.
1943. ARTHUR CORRIE KEEP, M.D.
1944. THOMAS PERCY LEGG, C.M.G., M.S.
1952. W. E. TANNER, M.S.
1953. J. SEYMOUR MAYNARD, M.D.
1954. T. JENNER HOSKIN, M.D.
1956. SEPTIMUS PHILIP SUNDERLAND
1957. A. HOPE-GOSSE, M.D.
1958. R. J. McNEILL LOVE, M.S.
1964. CHARLES WHEEN.

Index

135